The World of MODEL TRAINS

The World of MODEL TRAINS

Edited by
Patrick Whitehouse & Allen Levy

Bison Books

Published by
Bison Books Ltd.
176 Old Brompton Road
London, SW5
England

ISBN 0 86124 009 X

Printed in Hong Kong

Reprinted 1985

CONTENTS

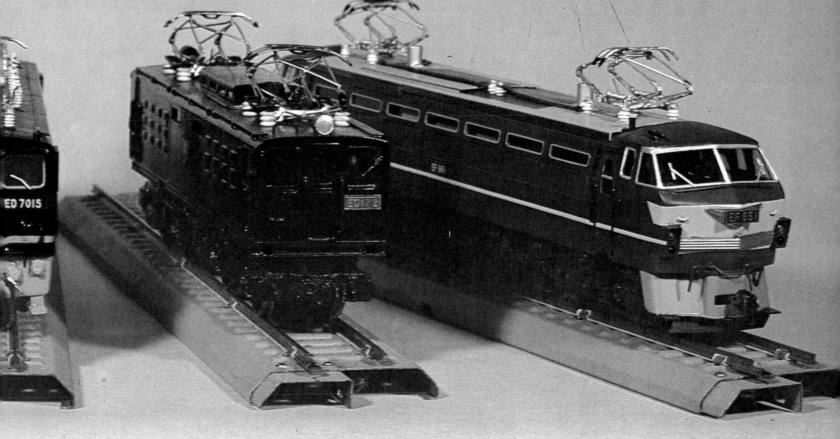

INTRODUCTION

This book does not claim to be anything new in the field of model railway literature; it does, however, tell something of the story of how the hobby has progressed over the past century. Ever since George Stephenson produced the *Rocket* the steam engine has proved to be an evocative monster which has had an enthusiastic following the world over; almost immediately embryo locomotive manufacturers provided prototype models as examples of their skills, to promote sales and this trend was followed over the years by their successors. Some fine models of great historic interest have found their way into collections and museums over the years.

But it was not until around the turn of the century that model railways in the form we know them today began to emerge and even then it was only the rich who could afford the better specimens — or perhaps any at all. The interwar years saw the development of the hobby and the beginning of its becoming one of the larger leisure activities for men and boys of all ages. This period also brought about the introduction of scale modelling in the popular sense — previously it was the commercial toymakers who made the running. That is not to say that the famous firms such as Marklin,

Bing, Bassett-Lowke, Hornby, Lionel & Ives did not play their part — they did but the serious modellers wanted something better. With the introduction of the smaller 4 mm and 3.5 mm scales — from the 1950s onwards by far the most popular of sizes — it became possible to build real railway models and with the coming of N and Z gauges, real landscapes, too. So vast has the hobby now become that almost any aspect can be followed, in time scale, prototype operation, scenic modelling, electronics and automatic working, steam, clockwork and electric — it is all there for the asking — or at least for the paying. Commercial manufacturers today cater not only for those who require a toy train set but also for the many who want to improve it and move towards a scale layout. Their products comprise locomotives, rolling stock and accessories of standard gauge or narrow for most parts of the Western world. Today it is a hobby that can suit all tastes and all pockets. This book examines a cross section of it all, the intriguing history, how it is done and above all how others have done it: lastly it looks at the new side of the hobby — collecting and by so doing learning something of the early history and early skills.

Both publisher and editor would like

to thank all those who have contributed; Allen Levy, whose book *A Century of Model Trains* has proved to be the bible for those interested in the history of commercial model trains and in collecting them, the two British magazines, *The Railway Modeller* and *The Model Railway Constructor* for permission to use photographs published within their pages and for advice, to Brian Monaghan for his excellent pictures and Paul Towers for his help, in particular with narrow gauge matters. Some pictures and written material were compiled and collected while researching for the partwork *History of Model and Miniature Railways* for the New English Library and this is hereby acknowledged. Our appreciation is also recorded to those individual modellers who have constructed the magnificent layouts and individual models depicted here and to the clubs without whom much knowledge and skills now available to individuals would be sadly missing. New Cavendish Books have made available certain rare items including commercial catalogues and Martin Hedges has edited the copy.

P. B. Whitehouse
February 1978

Above: The Blue train of the Japanese National Railways is an HO scale model. The head engine is a Class EF65. The second car which has the pantographs is the electric power and passengers' baggage car. The train consists of sleeping cars.

Below: This Hudson type locomotive in HO scale is a Class C60 passenger engine which was altered from Class C59 in 1953.

Chapter 1
HISTORY

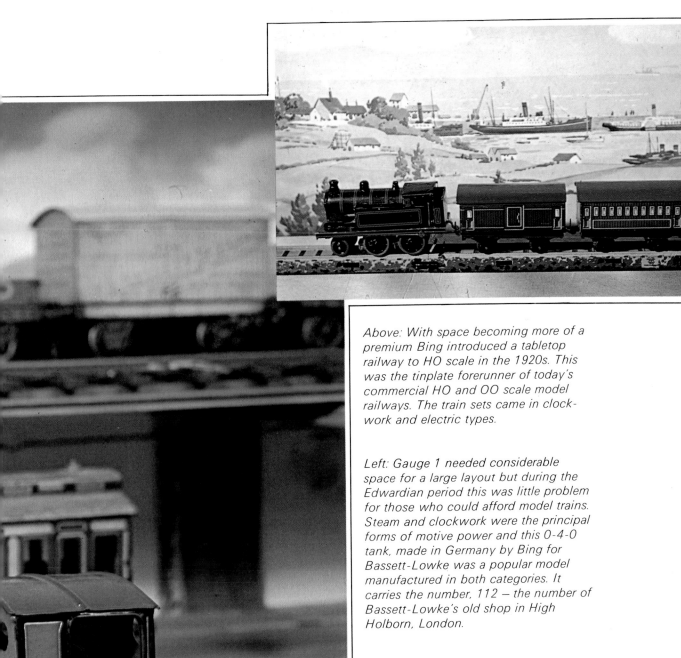

Above: With space becoming more of a premium Bing introduced a tabletop railway to HO scale in the 1920s. This was the tinplate forerunner of today's commercial HO and OO scale model railways. The train sets came in clockwork and electric types.

Left: Gauge 1 needed considerable space for a large layout but during the Edwardian period this was little problem for those who could afford model trains. Steam and clockwork were the principal forms of motive power and this 0-4-0 tank, made in Germany by Bing for Bassett-Lowke was a popular model manufactured in both categories. It carries the number, 112 — the number of Bassett-Lowke's old shop in High Holborn, London.

Below: A Bing tinplate station for use with table-top layouts. Note clips on the bottom of the platform for fixing to tracks.

Traditionally model railways were described as 'elementary mechanical toys, designed ostensibly to encourage the enthusiasm of youth', but invariably they became the extension of adult fantasy and fascination. At the risk of being criticised by eager market research analysts, one would hazard a guess (aided by statistics taken in the USA some years ago) that today the majority of model railway equipment is purchased by adults throughout the world and that over an average lifespan more model railway items are played with or operated by 'non-juveniles' than juveniles. To extend the argument it could be said that this has been the case since ready-to-run equipment became widely available after the turn of the century.

Model railways did not, however, begin like this and indeed the first model trains were used to support serious scientific experiments. As early as 1784 William Murdoch produced a Grasshopper Beam Single Vertical Cylinder steam locomotive to demonstrate his ideas to prospective investors. Later a more remarkable model was built by Timothy Hackworth, depicting his original design for the *Sans Pareil* of 1826, and was a fully operating $4\frac{1}{4}$-inch gauge model, although it is doubtful whether it ever ran on track. According to Gustav Reder, the model railway historian, the first working small scale model railway has been traced to his native Spain, and comprised a little spirit-fired steam locomotive some 13 inches long, which transported dolls around an exotic garden in Jerez de la Frontera. This railway, however, was primarily designed as a serious proposition for transporting sherry and because of its serious intent could not rightly be called a plaything. The railway that appears to qualify for the title of the first toy railway was built at St Cloud for the infant Prince Imperial of France around 1860.

As railways developed in the middle part of the 19th century, so replicas of

Below and right: Robert A. Lee's 1870 catalogue. This company is typical of the many ironmongers and opticians who sold models in the central London district before the turn of the century. A great many opticians in the Oxford Street area of London were noted for this type of trade and indeed many of the models were produced by instrument makers as ancillary lines. The primitive locomotives represent the archetype 'Dribbler' or 'Piddler' as they were most popularly known.

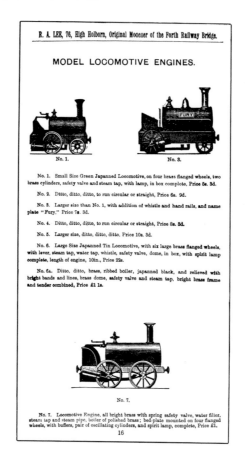

Below: A typically American wooden floor train of the late 19th century. These trains were marvellously decorated with lithographed paper, a process rarely used in Europe.

their existence came to be manufactured. In their very crudest form, these were hand-coloured, stamped representations similar to the early flat hand-painted tin soldiers or merely decorated wooden pull trains. Later these were cast in lead which gave them slightly more detail and relief. There is evidence to suggest that as early as 1826 a non-powered toy locomotive was put out by the Nuremburg firm of Mathias Hess, although there is no printed contemporary information on the actual hardware. Throughout history the engine or locomotive has always been the most glamorous manifestation of the railway and, of course, to qualify for the definition of locomotive, the contrivance needed to move under its own power. Logically, steam would provide this first powering of a model locomotive as the real technology was being developed at a rapid pace on the many railways of the time. Around 1862 a catalogue issued by the London firm of Joseph Myers describes a little oscillating cylinder locomotive as a commercial offering. Oscillating cylinders became the earliest method of powering a small scale locomotive as they were cheap to manufacture in that there were no valves or complicated linkages. Several million of these little engines with either a 2-2-0 or 2-2-2 wheel arrangement would flood the market over the next 30 years. Made principally in England and France and to a lesser extent in Nuremburg, they became popularly known as 'dribblers'. Whereas these early examples were primarily made in brass, it was the Nuremburg toy industry that graduated to the true mass production of toy steam engines in tinplate and pressed sheet metal.

In America the old tinsmiths of Bristol, who had emigrated to New England, produced non-powered floor trains of the most imaginative designs. They were hand-painted and often displayed fantastic transfers more appropriate to the pottery industry than to toy trains. This strange delicate period was to disappear

THE "GOLDEN GATE SPECIAL."

Extreme left: Hornby were probably the best known firm in the commercial model train market during the inter-war years. Hornby trains were all made in that famous factory in Binns Road, Liverpool and the company set out to produce not only boxed train sets, but a complete working railway system. Each year from 1925/26 Hornby published a new illustrated catalogue, The Hornby Book of Trains, *in full colour. Today these are collectors' items.*

Below: No 2 Special – a Hornby clockwork model of the LNER 4-4-0 No 234 Yorkshire. *Prior to the introduction of the LMS* Princess Elizabeth *Pacific in 1937/38 these No 2 Special locomotives were the only true-to-type engines.*

No. 296 ·· THE "PRINCE."

A Locomotive Engine and Tender on 8 wheels, Coupled Drivers and Bogie Truck in front, Polished Bright Brass Boiler, 7 in. long, 2¼ in. diameter, with Longitudinal stay bolt from end to end, 2 cast Rings shrunk on round the boiler, making the boiler very strong and safe, Steam Dome, Ramsbottom Safety Valve, Funnel, Bell Whistle, Regulator, Gauge Tap, Cab, Signal Lamp, Buffers, Hand Rails, Coupling Chain, Splashers, 2 Eccentrics, with automatic reversing motion, Connecting Rods, Steam Pipes, Spirit Lamp, 2 correct pattern slide Valve Cylinders, ⅝ in. bore, 1 in. stroke, will run backwards or forwards, circular or straight, on a floor or rail, Tender on 6 wheels with Springs, Axle Boxes, Buffers, Coupling Chain, Brake Handle and Tank inside, the whole 18 in. in length, painted and lined in colours, all parts screwed together. *Our own make from brass and steel castings.* Gauge 2⅜ in., price £4 10s. 0d.

Circular Tin Rail 17/- (see page 57). Circular Iron Rail 20 ft. in circumference, mounted on strong wood base, 30/- (see page 57).

Polished Mahogany Wood Carriages 13/6 and 15/6. Guard's Vans 15/6. Trucks 10/6 and 12/-. Brake Vans 13/6. (See page 56), to suit either of the Locomotives, Nos. 293, 294, 296.

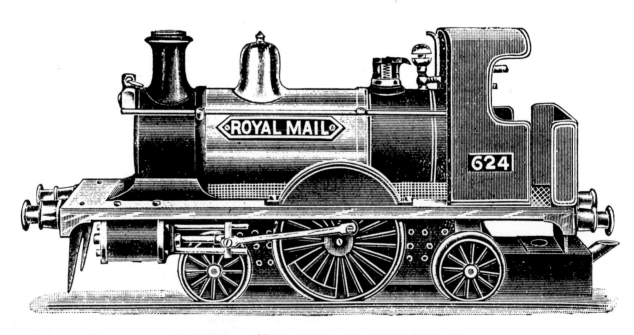

No. 297 ·· THE "ROYAL MAIL."

A Locomotive Engine on 6 wheels, Polished Bright Brass Boiler, 8½ in. long, 2½ in. diameter, with Longitudinal stay bolt from end to end, 2 cast Rings shrunk on round the boiler, making the boiler very strong and safe, Steam Dome, Bell, Whistle, Ramsbottom Safety Valve, 2 Gauge Taps, Regulator, Signal Lamp, Buffers, Line Clearers, Hand Rails, Coupling Chain, Cab, Splashers, 2 Eccentrics with automatic reversing motion, Steam Pipes, Connecting Rods, 2 correct pattern Slide Valve Cylinders, ¾ in. bore, 1⅛ in. stroke, will run backwards or forwards, circular or straight, on a floor or rails, all parts screwed together, total length 15½ in., painted and lined in colours. *Our own make from brass and steel castings.* Price £4 5s. 0d. This Engine fitted with Bogie Carriage and eight Wheels, 10/- extra.

Circular Rail 25 ft. in circumference, mounted on strong wood base, price £1 17s. 6d. (see page 57). Polished Mahogany wood Carriages and Guard's Vans 20/- each. Trucks 12/6 and 15/6 each. Brake Vans 15/6 each (see page 56).

at the turn of the century when the on-slaught of mass-produced German toy trains would reach America and their own indigenous industry would get under way as part of the great American industrial revolution, making folk art processes obsolete. While the 'dribbler' and its more sophisticated fixed cylinder derivatives were being perfected in England and France, the Bavarian clock-making industry centred around the Nuremburg region in Germany gave birth to the clockwork-powered toy, and one of the principal recipients of this clean and safe means of propulsion was the toy train. It was from about this time in the 1870s that the ponderous and relatively expensive brass live-steam loco-motive went into decline and it also heralded the dawn of Nuremburg as one of the most prolific toy-making centres in the world. Despite the trend towards simple toys, two German manufacturers of the late 19th century stand out for their exotic approach to the model steam engine.

It must be remembered that at this time even though toy trains were widely available they were aimed at a burgeoning and relatively affluent middle class, and it was not unusual for the price of a fairly sophisticated live-steam locomotive in the late 19th century to be in the region of £10 to £15 which, at that time, could

Above: Floor Train — an early Schoenner model based on American practice.

Far left: Early British fixed-cylinder steam engines. These were among the first of the more sophisticated models of the late 19th century, from Steven's model dockyard.

Below: Schoenner's masterpiece in 3-inch gauge was this SECR 4-4-0 in live steam was loosely based on Wain-wright's classic D-type locomotive. This locomotive was listed in Bassett-Lowke's catalogue, around 1904 and although it could hardly have been a mass-produced item in view of its relatively high cost (eight guineas), nonetheless, several examples have come to light in recent years. There is no evidence that that manufacturer produced SECR coaches for this locomotive, surprising in view of the fact that they produced Great Central coaches without apparently producing a Great Central locomotive.

represent the annual wage of a vast number of manual workers. Into this world of late Victorian affluence came the products of two manufacturers in particu-lar, namely Jean Schoenner, founded in 1875 and Georges Carette, who followed in 1888. Carette went on to become one of the largest toy manufacturers in Nuremburg while Schoenner remained rela-tively small. Both of these firms produced top-of-the-line steam locomotives that now appear high on the list of model railway exotica, and are greatly sought after by collectors.

If there are peaks and troughs in the story, then from the last decade of the 19th century until the first of the 20th would comprise the first of those peaks. In view of later events, it was ironic that both Schoenner and Carette, and indeed that most of their competitors, directed their efforts to the English market which appeared to have the spending power, love of railways and — probably more important — a naissant love of hobbies and pastimes. Initially, as agents of this production, Messrs Bassett-Lowke were to be the prime catalysts in the marketing and distribution of German-made model railway equipment. In that firm's early catalogues commencing in 1901, the beautiful 3-inch gauge SECR 4-4-0 live-steam locomotive by Schoenner, a superb mixture of brass and pressed tinplate,

could be seen. Also illustrated was an extraordinary Schoenner Adams LSWR 4-4-0 which even today eludes collectors. Probably produced in minute quantities, one or two must surely lurk in the dusty lofts of some large households in England or its one-time colonies! The fascination of the pursuit, collection and maintenance of old toy trains is a subject in itself and will be touched upon in a later chapter.

At about the same time Carette also produced an extraordinary range of locomotives principally for the English market and among these The Lady of the Lake and GNR Single locomotives were the star attractions. The Lady of the Lake, a live-steam model, was relatively simple in body and finish, with oscillating cylinders, but it was remarkable in that it was probably one of the first true-to-type commercial models ever offered. The GNR Single incorporated two fixed double-acting patent slide-valve cylinders with reversing gear of unparalleled complexity. Extensive use of castings made this the least likely model to win any speed or efficiency trials. For the American market Carette produced a stunning replica of Vauclain's classic Compound No. 2350 and again it incorporated all his trickery including simulated inside valve gears (so much a feature of the real locomotive) and a

Above: One of the first true-to-type models ever made – the Carrette Lady of the Lake *marketed by Bassett-Lowke at the turn of the century.*

Below: Carrette's famous Vauclain Compound, marketed by Bassett-Lowke in 1904 in both steam and clockwork, was infinitely superior in appearance to anything being manufactured in America at that time. It is probably one of Carette's most desirable models for the clockwork version featured a simulated internal valve gear.

patent 'Coulisse' reversing system. Schoenner, too, was preoccupied with the American market and before the turn of the century produced some amazing floor trains, mainly for live steam but also including the classic New York Central & Hudson River Rail Road No. 2990, probably the finest lithographed tinplate floor train ever made. The largest example of this had a track width of $3\frac{1}{2}$ inches. While Schoenner and Carette were two of the more glamorous firms of this time, they were not to survive and by the end of the First World War they had both disappeared.

This period saw the establishment of two of the most legendary names in

Model "New York Central" Express Steam Locomotives.

A S will be seen by illustration, this is a Model of one of the celebrated American Express Locomotives. It has a strong Brass Boiler, Double-action Slide-valve Cylinders with exhaust into Funnel, Reversing from Cab, Safety Valve, Bell Whistle, Water Gauge and Stop-cock, Spirit Tank in Tender, four-wheeled Bogie Carriages and eight-wheeled Tender.

The whole Loco. is complete with all details as illustrated, also Cow Catcher, and excellently enamelled.

No. 1—$1\frac{3}{4}$ in. gauge, 22 in. long over all   ...   .   Price £3 15 6

model trains, namely Gebrüder Bing and Gebrüder Marklin, both of whom were firmly established in Nuremburg by the turn of the century. Marklin are still very much in business today making model trains and scenery and we shall meet up with this firm and their products as the story unfolds.

An early form of propulsion was the impulse created by a flywheel. A relatively heavy flywheel set in a light tin body could be wound up on the string of a pulley and then the whirring contraption would be placed on the floor. The effect of the friction between the flywheel and shaft gave it sufficient impetus to drive the locomotive for a reasonable length of time on a flat surface. Clearly this system was of little use for a working railway, but nonetheless very suitable for the nursery. Indeed this type of toy model train was remarkably popular right up to the 1930s.

Shortly after the widespread adoption of steam for indoor trains came clockwork. The oldest known surviving example was marketed in 1867 by Baker, an instrument maker in London and this, like all clockwork trains, derived its mechanism from the basic technology of clockmaking. It is to the Nuremburg area that one looks for the first large scale clockwork train makers, and they included Gunthermann and Hess to whom reference has been made. The French also made very delicate tinplate floor trains, some of which had simple clockwork motors, others of which were merely meant to be pulled along on a string. Maltète et Parent and Dessin produced some outstanding examples in France before and shortly after the turn of the century. Many of these are still displayed by collectors.

In America, once again deriving from the clockmaking industry in Connecticut, came the George W. Brown Company at Forestville. Their locomotives included the fantasy types referred to earlier and while they were true locomotives in that they were self-propelled, it was Ives who became the first giant on the American clockwork railway scene. Initially their trains were tinplate, but gradually they were superceded by the exceptional North American predilection for cast iron. Perhaps the fact that the Americans were not natural exporters of toy trains enabled them to indulge themselves in this way. But think of the problems of the poor Nuremburg companies who later were forced to follow this fashion and freight tons of cast iron American-outline trains across the Atlantic! At this time also, an indigenous American live-steam train industry had emerged, albeit on a much smaller scale than its European counterpart. Eugene Beggs and later John Garlick produced a range of $1\frac{7}{8}$-inch

Above: A typical late 19th century American floor train, put out by Althof Bergmann. Trains such as these had very close links with American folk art in which the locomotive has always been an important ingredient. Nothing as fanciful as these trains was made in Europe and they stand in sharp contrast to the somewhat brutal functionalism of the American toy and model trains that superseded them at the turn of the century.

gauge oscillating cylinder locomotives and, indeed, this was almost akin to gauge 1, which later became one of the most popular early commercial gauges in Europe. Beggs engines were unique in one other respect: the axles were offset in such a way that the locomotive would run easily upon a pre-determined fixed radius. Beggs also marketed a unique, if not particularly elegant rail system which comprised vertical steel strips sunk into solid continuous slotted sleepers. At the time when American toys were among the heaviest ever made for their size, Beggs was manufacturing coaches made of pasteboard and decorated with litho papers, and these must surely qualify as some of the lightest toy trains ever made, weighing next to nothing.

Early trains were clockwork or steam and were designed to run primarily on whatever flat surface was available. Only later were they adapted for running on rails. With the coming of model railways on tracks came the desire to have the facility to reverse the locomotive (oscillating cylinder locomotives are not reversible). For a steam engine this meant simple slip eccentric reversing, i.e. placing a heavy hand on the boiler and literally centring the eccentrics by pushing the locomotive backwards, thereby reversing the sequence of steam into the fixed cylinders through the valves. A further refinement was, of course, reversing the valve sequence via a lever in the cab or, more normally in the first of these 'advanced' types, by the horizontal movement of a lever protruding from the side of the splasher or cab. Initially clockwork locomotives were non-reversing, but later a reversing ratchet was incorporated enabling the motor first to be put into neutral and then reversed. Model trains entered the world of true-to-life trains.

The first known tracks for model trains were bent sections of brass secured to wooden sleepers and as the industry progressed mass production techniques were brought to bear on this most important aspect of the system. Sleepers were stamped out and clipped by a series of tabs to the rolled rail section, which in itself was an extruded pressing. Obviously in the beginning track was only manufactured in two-rail as rails were not required to act as conductors for the 'magic' innovative properties of electrical current.

The next great phase in model railways was the battle of the gauges. By the late 19th century, the world had come to adopt 4 feet $8\frac{1}{2}$ inches as the most widely accepted full-size gauge, and while the question of gauge and scale is dealt with at a later point, here we might look at this question in a purely historic perspective. Marklin were to set the pace in standardisation of the main commercial gauges

No. 503.

No. 0.—Best Quality Locomotive, with Tender, fitted with long Oxydized Brass Boiler, Turned Brass Wheels, Oscillating Cylinders, Steam Whistle, Safety Valve and Dome.   12in. long, including Tender.   **1¼in. Gauge.**   8/3

No. 1.—Ditto, 16in. long.   **1¾in. Gauge.**   10/6

No. 2.—Ditto, 17in. long.   **2in. Gauge.**   14/6

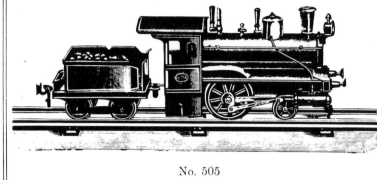

No. 505

No. 1.—Best Quality Locomotive with Oxydized Brass Boiler, turned Brass Wheels, pair of Double Action Slide Valve Cylinders (Patent), Whistle, Safety Valve, Dome and Starting tap.   16in. long.   **1¾in. Gauge.**   14/6

No. 2.—Ditto, 17in. long.   **2in. Gauge.**   20/6

No. 3.—Ditto, 24in. long.   **2½in. Gauge.**   47/6

which initially were O gauge – 35 mm, gauge 2 – 54 mm and gauge 3 – 75 mm. In order to gain some idea of the comparison, this company's circle of track required 6 pieces for O gauge, 8 pieces for gauge 1 and 12 pieces for gauges 2 and 3. Obviously the radii necessary to achieve circles of track using approximately 14-inch lengths did not begin to concern itself with scale, and it must be remembered that the manufacturer's chief concern was to sell as big a railway system as possible to fit within the confines of a domestic setting, notwithstanding that far more space was available in those days. Marklin went ahead to produce the first known points and this also was the key to the idea of expanding a model railway. Both Marklin and Bing produced a staggering array of tinplate accessories and indeed, the hand-painted stations (invariably lit by real candles), signals, tunnels and engine sheds were to emphasise that marriage of folk art and the commercial process which was to form the basis for the collectability of so much of this material in later years. Virtually everything in these early days was hand-painted, but Marklin also widely used the stencil to apply exotic lettering detail on their coaches and wagons e.g. *Compagnie des Wagons Lits et des Grands Express European. Papier-maché* and plaster passengers sat impaled on spikes, their hand-painted faces gleaming with content.

Far and away the most prolific type of locomotive, marketed by all the principal German manufacturers of this time was the single wheel 'storkleg' type, and Bing, Carette, Schoenner, Plank and Falk

Above: Typical 'storkleg' locomotives of the late 19th and early 20th century. This predominantly German design replaced the earlier brass 'dribblers' and judging by the number that have survived, were presumably made in exceedingly large quantities.

Right: Voltamp was one of the earliest manufacturers to market electric-powered model trains, and this was later to become the universal means of toy train propulsion. Illustrated here are three pages outlining Voltamp's main offerings in 1911.

all offered very similar ranges. Marklin, for some reason, eschewed this phase, although they were known to have produced single wheel clockwork locomotives. There are no accurate records for the size of this market, but in view of the number of these types that have survived, it must have been considerable.

Once the model railways had been accepted by the public as a recurring purchase and no mere novelty, the manufacturers applied themselves to the process of improvement and innovation, safe in the knowledge that next season would produce another substantial crop of purchasers plus existing customers enlarging last year's train set. In fact model railways can claim to be the longest-running mechanical toy in retail selling terms, and indeed have been the mainstay of the hobby and toy store for over three-quarters of a century. Perhaps the fact that trains run on pre-determined but endlessly flexible trackways is the key to this continued popularity. Furthermore they are the only toys wherein the essential quality of the real object can be reduced to a totally controlled and working system within a relatively small space. It is simply not possible to do this with aeroplanes, motor cars or ships as the former require unlimited airspace and therefore some form of highly sophisticated remote control and the latter simply lose realism by being run on pre-set trackways or being set in ponds and rivers surrounded by out of scale water movements. All the developments so far were merely a minor overture to the big breakthrough that would establish model railways as a universal and almost time-

VOLTAMP TROLLEY—Double Truck

Built Only for Standard 2-Inch Gauge Track

6 Volts
¾ Ampere
Battery
or Street
Current

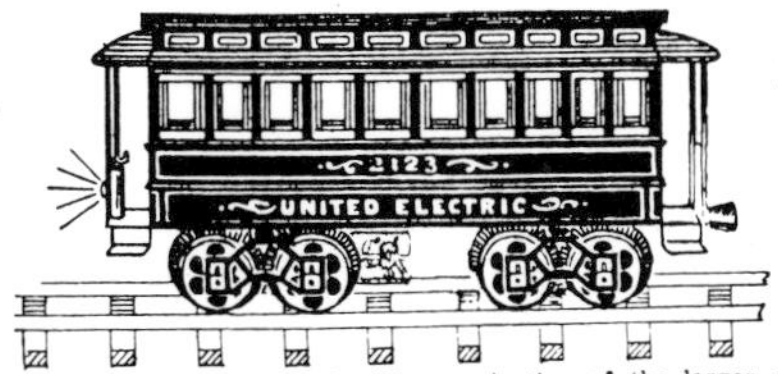

Electric
Headlight

Price
$6.00

The Double-Truck Trolley is a splendid reproduction of the larger cars used in the big cities. The trucks are carefully balanced and centrally bolted to the platform. The **Motor** is coupled to both axles of the forward truck by a set of four heavy brass gears and a steel pinion, an arrangement by which **both axles are driven** equally, insuring a steady and powerful pull on level grade or hill. This car will haul one or more Trailers over a 7 per cent. grade at good speed, using only 6 to 8 Volts of Battery or Street Current.

The **Body** is made similar to the single-truck Trolley, with a neat finish in maroon and white, gold stripes and lettering.

The addition of an **Electric Headlight** to all VOLTAMP railways lends a decided realistic effect. The lamp is made especially for headlight purposes, and has a reflector back which throws the rays over considerable space.

Specifications.—6 to 8 Volts, ¾ Ampere. Speed about 175 feet per minute. Length 14½ in., width 3½ in., height 5¾ in., weight 3¼ lbs. Has 10 windows on each side, two long seats, Electric Headlight and rear coupler to carry Trailers. Will take any curve of 15-in. radius and over. **Controller-Reverser.**

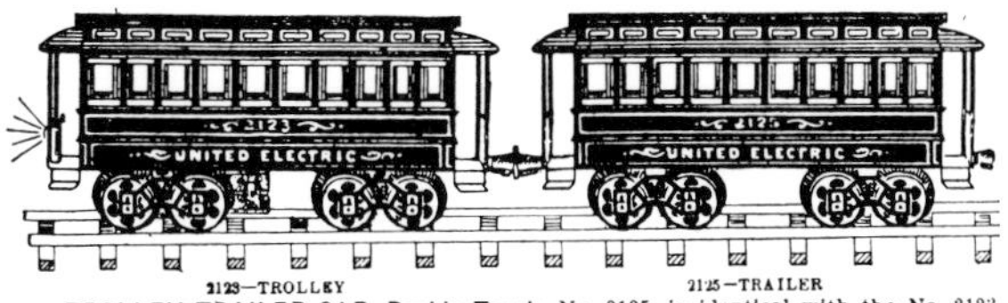

2123—TROLLEY 2125—TRAILER

TROLLEY TRAILER CAR, Double Truck, No. 2125, is identical with the No. 2123 Trolley, but has no Motor or Controller-Reverser. Automatic Couplers.

List No.		Price
2123	Double-Truck Trolley, weight packed 4¾ lbs.	$6.00
2124	Double-Truck TROLLEY, with 9 ft. Steel Track, Ties, Connector; weight packed 6 lbs.	6.35
2125	Double-Truck TROLLEY TRAILER, weight packed 3½ lbs.	2.50
2192	Extra Brushes, per set of 3, **prepaid, 15 cts.**; 2 sets, **prepaid**	.25
2408	Extra Reflector Lamp for Headlight, 6 Volts, **prepaid**	.35
2228	**Equipment.**—No. 2123 Trolley, No. 2150 9-ft. Coppered Steel Track and Ties (6-ft. Circle), No. 2154 Connector, No. 1316 Battery of 4 Dry Cells in case with Switch; weight packed about 25 lbs.	7.35
2229	**Equipment**—No. 2123 Trolley, No. 2125 Trailer, No. 2159 or No. 2163 Track and Ties, No. 2154 Connector, No. 2:64 Bridge, No. 1317 Battery of 6 Dry Cells and Switch; length of train 30 in.; weight packed about 35 lbs.	11.50

NOTE.—No. 2123 Trolley, fitted with a **Relay-Reverser,** extra charge **$2.50.** The value of this attachment is instantly appreciated. The switch may be placed any distance away from the track, yet the car will be sent forward or backward as the operator wills. Works perfectly on Battery or Direct Lighting current

MINING ENGINE — TUNNEL MOTOR

6 Volts
¾ Ampere
Battery or
Street
Current

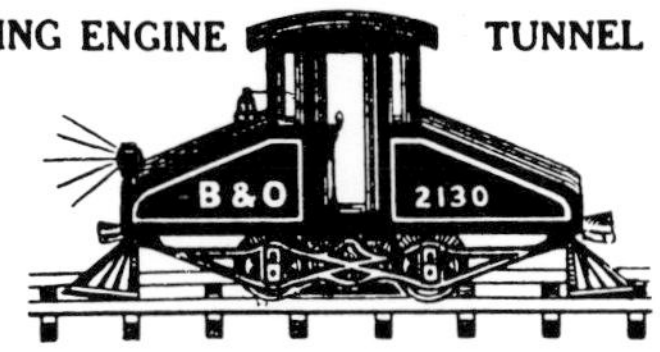

Electric
Headlight

Price
$4.50

This is the boy's delight, and not without reason. It is more than a mere toy—a model—and will lead the young mind to think over and study the fundamental problems of railroading, at the same time affording boundless pleasure because of its realistic appearance and remarkable work. Coupled to a train of three or more cars, it proves an attraction for children that surpasses all other amusement.

The Motor arrangements are similar to the Single-Truck Trolley. Like the latter, it is triple-geared, has excellent pull, sufficient to haul with ease the four freight cars shown below on even or 7 per cent. hill grade. A **Controller-Reverser** is placed conveniently in the cab, and a slight movement of the lever will send the engine forward or backward, start or stop it. Finished in steel-blue color, with gold lettering and stripes.

Specifications.—6 to 8 Volts, ¾ Ampere. Speed about 150 feet per minute. Length over all 10½ in., width 3½ in., height 5¾ in., weight 3 lbs. Has **Electric Headlight** and Swinging Bell, and carries Cowcatcher on both ends, with couplers to haul Trailers.

List No.	**Built Only for Standard 2-Inch Gauge Track**	Price
2130	MINING ENGINE, Single Truck; weight packed about 4¼ lbs.	$4.50
2131	MINING ENGINE, Single Truck, with 9 ft. Track, Ties and Connector; weight packed about 5½ lbs.	4.85
2408	Extra Lamp for Headlight, 6 Volts	.35

NOTE.—No. 2130 Mining Engine, fitted with a **Relay Reverser,** extra charge **$2.50.**

For EQUIPMENTS see page 98

2166
2191

2192
2193

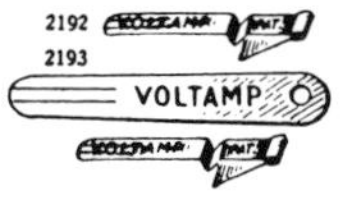

2126

2127

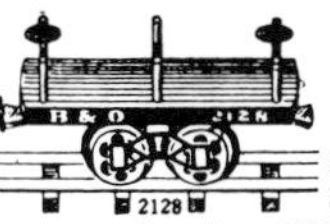

2128

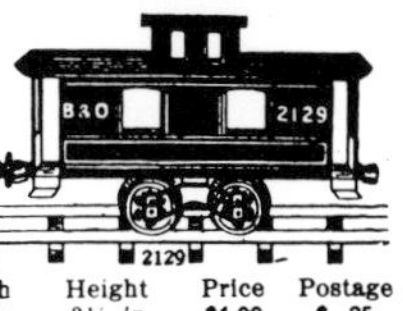

2129

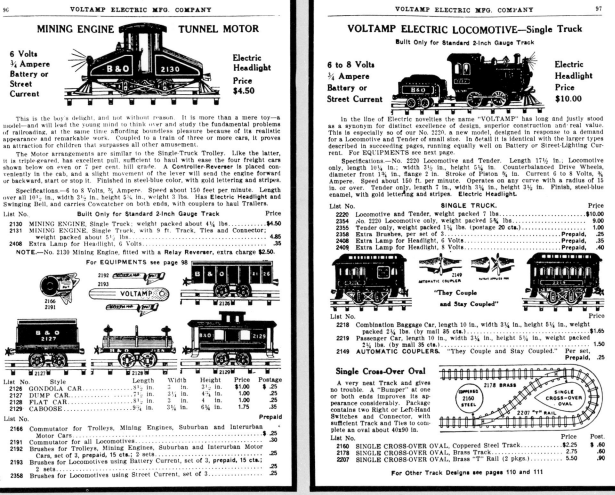

List No.	Style	Length	Width	Height	Price	Postage
2126	GONDOLA CAR	8½ in.	3 in.	3½ in.	$1.00	$ .25
2127	DUMP CAR	7½ in.	3¼ in.	4¾ in.	1.00	.25
2128	FLAT CAR	8½ in.	3 in.	4 in.	1.00	.25
2129	CABOOSE	9¾ in.	3¼ in.	6¼ in.	1.75	.35

List No.		Prepaid
2166	Commutator for Trolleys, Mining Engines, Suburban and Interurban Motor Cars	$ .25
2191	Commutator for all Locomotives	.30
2192	Brushes for Trolleys, Mining Engines, Suburban and Interurban Motor Cars, set of 3, **prepaid, 15 cts.**; 2 sets	.25
2193	Brushes for Locomotives using Battery Current, set of 3, **prepaid, 15 cts.**; 2 sets	.25
2358	Brushes for Locomotives using Street Current, set of 3	.25

VOLTAMP ELECTRIC LOCOMOTIVE—Single Truck

Built Only for Standard 2-Inch Gauge Track

6 to 8 Volts
¾ Ampere
Battery or
Street Current

Electric
Headlight
Price
$10.00

In the line of Electric novelties the name "VOLTAMP" has long and justly stood as a synonym for distinct excellence of design, superior construction and real value. This is especially so of our No. 2220, a new model, designed in response to a demand for a Locomotive and Tender of small size. In detail it is identical with the larger types described in succeeding pages, running equally well on Battery or Street-Lighting Current. For EQUIPMENTS see next page.

Specifications.—No. 2220 Locomotive and Tender. Length 17½ in.; Locomotive only, length 10¼ in.; width 3½ in., height 5¼ in. Counterbalanced Drive Wheels, diameter front 1¾ in., flange 2 in. Stroke of Piston ¾ in. Current 6 to 8 Volts, ¾ Ampere. Speed about 150 ft. per minute. Operates on any curve with a radius of 15 in. or over. Tender only, length 7 in., width 3¼ in., height 3½ in. Finish, steel-blue enamel, with gold lettering and stripes. **Electric Headlight.**

List No.	**SINGLE TRUCK.**	Price
2220	Locomotive and Tender, weight packed 7 lbs.	$10.00
2354	No. 2220 Locomotive only, weight packed 5¾ lbs.	9.00
2355	Tender only, weight packed 1¼ lbs. (postage **20 cts.**)	1.00
2358	Extra Brushes, per set of 3 ... Prepaid,	.25
2408	Extra Lamp for Headlight, 6 Volts ... Prepaid,	.35
2409	Extra Lamp for Headlight, 8 Volts ... Prepaid,	.40

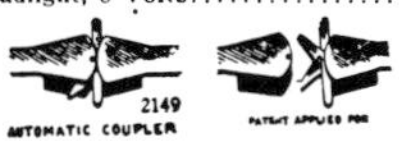

"They Couple and Stay Coupled"

List No.		Price
2218	Combination Baggage Car, length 10 in., width 3¼ in., height 5¼ in., weight packed 2¼ lbs. (by mail **35 cts.**)	$1.65
2219	Passenger Car, length 10 in., width 3¼ in., height 5¼ in., weight packed 2¼ lbs. (by mail **35 cts.**)	1.50
2149	**AUTOMATIC COUPLERS.** "They Couple and Stay Coupled." Per set, **Prepaid,**	.25

Single Cross-Over Oval

A very neat Track and gives no trouble. A "Bumper" at one or both ends improves its appearance considerably. Package contains two Right or Left-Hand Switches and Connector, with sufficient Track and Ties to complete an oval about 40x90 in.

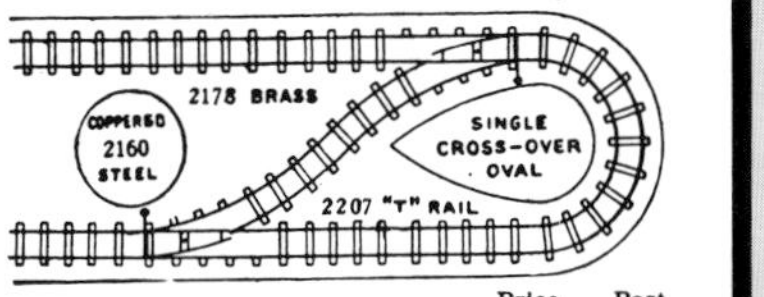

List No.		Price	Post.
2160	SINGLE CROSS-OVER OVAL, Coppered Steel Track	$2.25	$ .60
2178	SINGLE CROSS-OVER OVAL, Brass Track	2.75	.60
2207	SINGLE CROSS-OVER OVAL, Brass "T" Rail (2 pkgs.)	5.50	.90

For Other Track Designs see pages 110 and 111

No. 17. Coal Mining Locomotive and Dump Cars.

PRICE, $6.25.

5 to 6 VOLTS.   **¾ AMPERE.**

This equipment is the same as No. 3, but dump cars are substituted for the coal cars.

These cars are made so that they will stand upright and may be filled with sand, gravel, etc.

Each car can be dumped as desired. This train will be found of the greatest interest and will be a never failing source of pleasure and amusement.

Complete equipment consists of locomotive, three dump cars, 18 feet of 2 inch gauge strip steel track and four dry batteries.

Cars are made of cast iron, have metal bottoms and improved wheels. Are very durable.

Locomotive is the same as the No. 3 locomotive.

Length of train, 20 inches.

Weight complete, boxed, 13½ lbs.

Locomotive Only, $3.50 each.

Dump cars, 40 cents each. By mail, 50 cents.

Track and Ties (strip steel) in 9 ft. lengths, 35 cents.

Extra dry batteries, per cell, 25 cents.

Boston.

Gentlemen:

I want to tell you how much I appreciate your railways. I started five years ago by receiving the electric locomotive and passenger train for a Christmas present, and I have been adding to it until now I have nearly all the cars and engines there are. I have a whole room laid out with switches, cross-overs, barns, round house, and also a signal system with small incandescent lights in series. I take great pleasure in fixing automatic switches, etc.

Yours truly,
ROSS D. SAMPSON,
94 Essex St.

Above and right: Carlisle & Finch was another early manufacturer on the American toy railroad scene and, as in the case of Voltamp and the early English and French instrument makers, toy trains evolved as ancillary lines to their main manufacturing bases.

less pursuit — electricity.

Further mention will be made of electricity when dealing with the motive power of Thomas Davenport's first electric model train. The first full size electric railway was introduced by Siemens at the Berlin Exhibition in 1879 and from that moment forward it was inevitable that the toy makers would attempt to follow. However, unlike steam and clockwork, which enjoyed autonomous power sources, the electric motor required an outside source of supply. Battery technology was delayed for many decades before it advanced to the stage where models of any type could propel themselves while actually carrying batteries.

The Americans were the first to seize on the novelty of electric-powered toy trains and indeed their railways were the first to use electric trains in full public service. Initially the principal manufacturers confined electric propulsion to tramways as this was not asking the public to strain its imagination too far. A betting man might have argued that a massive industry built on putting electric motors into steam outline locomotives was unlikely to succeed. In fact in Europe this was for many years the case, although the American market embraced the electric train with enthusiasm and indeed no other form of model propulsion seriously competed with the electric train on that continent.

The development of electric trains in Europe was initially confined to models of contemporary electric locomotives such as the Central London Bo Bos and the early P & O locomotives that ran between Paris—Austerlitz and Paris—Orsay. Nonetheless, the realisation that live-steam locomotives needed careful handling, and usually the presence of an adult, and the restrictions of controlling a clockwork locomotive in full flight, led manufacturers to a greater awareness of the commercial possibilities of electric-powered toy trains. Thus as early as 1904 Marklin followed its American counterparts Carlisle and Finch, Knapp and Voltamp in producing electric-powered, steam outline locomotives in gauges O, 1 and 2. Something like a 40 to 60 volt supply was necessary to run these early locomotives and in Marklin's case this led to considerable lumps and bumps appearing round the locomotive, concealing bearings and bushes.

All early mains supply railways were of the three-rail variety (although simple two-rail battery examples appeared earlier). It is interesting to reflect on a contemporary expert's view of the problems involved with early electrical systems, particularly those related to obtaining a DC supply from AC mains:

> To obtain DC from AC mains, you could make up a chemical rectifier from four glass jars, in which stood aluminium and iron plates separated by wood or vulcanite; the jars were fitted with a saturated solution of ammonium phosphate, and then you could put your current through. Be careful though, or with three or four hours of overloading, the whole thing would start to boil.

This expert went on to relate how he cut

THE
CARLISLE & FINCH
COMPANY
CINCINNATI, OHIO, U.S.A.

REPRINT – 1915 CARLISLE & FINCH
ARTIC PRINTING COMPANY
2252 DIXIE HIGHWAY
PONTIAC, MICHIGAN 48055

C. & F. RY.

ELECTRICAL NOVELTIES, DYNAMOS, MOTORS, EXPERIMENTAL APPARATUS & GAS ENGINES.

corners by using an ordinary electric fire bar as the means of resistance between the controller and the mains and one can only gasp with horror at what might have been the result.

The European system required a centre third rail for current pick up and the electric motor invariably drove a central shaft which transmitted traction to the wheels via a strange 'U' section (similar to Hall cranks common on Austrian locomotives at that time) fixed to a four-wheel mechanism. Steam outlined electric-powered trains from Bing followed in 1908. Coupling rods were deliberately omitted from the early Bing engines, the final drive being located between the frames. Whereas the earliest electric toy trains worked successfully off primitive batteries serving current to the track, the great leap forward was the ability to have power direct from the house mains. The German manufacturers were placed in a difficult position concerning standards in view of the fact that the British authorities decided against the use of high voltage mains supply and so different systems evolved initially for the continental and English markets.

As more and more people became familiar with real railways, so the toy train maker was gradually forced into making his products look more like the real thing. Nobody in the history of model railways was more concerned and at the same time more responsible for the creation of scale appearance models than W. J. Bassett-Lowke. Born into a boiler-maker's family in Northampton, he was to be the man who, as so often in history, was in the right place at the right time with the drive and industry to bring ideas to reality. After visiting Paris for the Exposition in 1900, W. J. Bassett-Lowke struck up a liaison with Gebrüder Bing which was to set the standards for generations of model railway enthusiasts. From 1909, under the guidance of Henry Greenly, a legendary English model engineer, Bassett-Lowke placed orders with this giant German toy manufacturer for the production of English outline locomotives, rolling stock and coaches, the excellence of which was never to be surpassed in that medium. He had parallel arrangements with Carette and to a much lesser extent with Marklin, although after

Bing's demise in the late 1920s, Bassett-Lowke would use Marklin in the same role. A glance at the Bassett-Lowke model railway catalogue of, say, 1911 will show the fruits of his collaboration at its zenith. For many years the British public was not totally aware of this collaboration, which was understandable in view of the worsening relationship between the two countries; it nevertheless represented a perfect marriage of German industry and British style. This relationship did not, of course, totally exclude items of British manufacture, but it would be fair to say that prior to the advent of Hornby trains in 1920, other English manufacturers continued to be engineer oriented, i.e. Carson and Stuart Turner. The latter was purported to be responsible for Bassett-Lowke's famous kit for the Midland Railway Johnson 4-4-0 (see illustration).

In the pre-First World War period, the electric train did not gain any wide acceptance in England, and indeed most

Above: A splendid electric-powered version of Marklin's Penn Class 28 Pacific produced around 1912 for gauge 1. The Pullman car is by the same maker and of a similar date.

Right: Typical printed tin lineside buildings as listed by Ives in 1909.

Below: This extraordinary spirit fired, live steam locomotive for 3¼-inch gauge was sold either as a set of castings or as a complete model by Bassett-Lowke from 1904 onwards. It is one of the few commercial models to sport an all-cast tender, and legend has it that these castings were produced for Bassett-Lowke by the equally famous and still extant firm of Stuart Turner in Henley.

M. R. COMPOUND LOCOMOTIVE NO. 2631.

Length, over all, 3ft. 1in.   **Gauge 3¼in.**   ⅝in. Scale.   Weight of Engine and Tender 31½ lbs.

DESCRIPTION OF
⅝ SCALE M. R. COMPOUND LOCOMOTIVE, NO. 2631.
——:o:——

This Scale Model Locomotive, fully described in our M. R. Loco. Pamphlet (12 pages, post free, 2d.), is an entirely new departure from the usual run of this class of Model. It is the result of careful thought and numerous experiments, and is an honest, and we may say, without egotism, a successful attempt to bring a high-class, up-to-date, substantial, reliable, and well-constructed scale working Model within the reach of the many.

It is built entirely from castings, and the Foot Plate, Side Frames and every little sundry is supplied in the set.

We have designed this Loco. with the hope that many will build it up themselves, and for this reason we have made the set of Castings as complete as possible, there being over 130 castings in the set.

The Boiler of the Locomotive is a type well-known to the readers of the *Model Engineer*, being fitted with a down-comer and circulating tubes.

We always have some of these Loco. s in hand at our works, and we use the very same Castings as supplied to our Customers.

Price of complete Set of Castings and Parts for Engine and Tender, including Full Set of correct working Drawings £5 0 0
Complete and Finished Boiler 3 19 6
Complete Locomotive and Tender, as illustration, fitted with Spirit and Water Tank, Hand Force Pump, Steam Gauge, Water Gauge, Cylinder Drain Cocks, enamelled and lined in correct M. R. colours, and tested to 120 lbs pressure, 3 ft. 1 in. long, 3¼ gauge £25 0 0
We only build a Finished Locomotive to order.

We strongly advise all those interested in this Loco. to send 2d. in stamps for our fully-illustrated 12-page Pamphlet containing full particulars.

A customer of ours in writing of this Locomotive says :—

"It embodies all the improvements and abolishes all the disadvantages that have troubled Model Loco. Builders for years past."

of the classic Bing/Bassett-Lowke products were available only in clockwork, although in later years many were adapted for electric running.

In America, however, the turn of the century witnessed the establishment of Lionel who eventually won the battle of the gauges with Ives. Gauge O, 1¼ inch, scale 7 mm to 1 foot, seems to have achieved recognition early on in the development of model railways both in Europe and in America. The larger gauges, however, were less universally accepted. Ives plumped for gauge 1 whereas Lionel established its standard gauge as 2⅛ inches. When Lionel began to compete seriously with Ives' gauge O railways, so Ives belatedly challenged Lionel with its own 2⅛-inch gauge products. Other American manufacturers saw where the battle lines were forming and, not wishing to be oddballs in the marketplace, fell in with both O gauge and Lionel's standard gauge (Dorfan describing them as narrow and wide gauge). At about this time Lionel dropped its 4-4-0 steam outline locomotives and turned exclusively to electric outline types in order to underline its claim that the day of the toy train had passed. Lionel electric trains, the company claimed, were faithful reproductions of the equipment used on America's great electrified systems, the

No. 119
Covered Platform, 11½ x 3¾ Inches

No. 121
Glass Covered Platform, 18½ x 9½ Inches

No. 114   Passenger Station, 13½ x 6 Inches

No. 115   Freight Station, 10 x 5½ Inches

Ives TrainS

"IVES TOYS MAKE HAPPY BOYS"

Above: Cover picture of the 1928 Ives Trains catalogue illustrating their standard gauge items (2¼ inch) which were only made in quantity in North America.

Far right and overleaf: These Marklin locomotives were sold principally by Gamages of London in the 1920s and 1930s and represent the last types made by Marklin for the British market with the exception of four scale models made in conjunction with Bassett-Lowke. All these engines represent Marklin's continuing style of toy-like imagery with little regard for the actual locomotives portrayed. The Lord Nelson, in particular, was not a commercial success and possibly due to this failure, it is one of the rarest and most desirable of collector's items today.

only difference, it was claimed, between the real and the toy, was size. Probably Lionel was right in this assessment, although in later years it would return with a vengeance to the manufacture of O and standard gauge electric-powered steam outline trains. In 1918 American Flyer, the third in the great triumvirate of American toy train producers, went over to making electric versions in addition to its existing O gauge clockwork trains, and it, too, renounced steam outline types when it first produced standard gauge items in 1925. Apart from Lionel's famous O gauge Hudson of the 1930s, American toy trains, whether O gauge or standard gauge, always retained the essence of the toy rather than the model. Nothing that was produced by any of these three great American manufacturers was to rival the scale appearance of the best 1909 Bing/Bassett-Lowke products. Perhaps it was the naive quality of this period that made American toy trains so collectable in later years.

In Europe Marklin reflected this emphasis on the toy rather than the scale appearance, at least until the late 1920s. Whereas standard gauge, exclusively in electric, dominated the American model

train scene until the 1920s, gauge O, as in Europe, dominated model railways internationally during the inter-war years. Since North America enjoyed the widespread use of low voltage alternating current for general domestic purposes much earlier than Europe, electric trains could be run quite safely through transformers from the lighting supply. Steam outline 2-4-2 locomotives, displaying only the character if by no means the real outline or wheel arrangement of the real thing, were a widespread style for toy train makers in America at this time.

The end of the First World War heralded considerable change in social and domestic conditions, and these had their effect on model railways in Europe. The widespread introduction of domestic electricity led to the acceptance of electric steam outline trains as modellers were not to be denied their favourites. All the major steam outline locomotives were offered in clockwork and electric and to a lesser extent in steam. Domestic housing became smaller in scale, as the new white collar middle class migrated to the suburbs of the large cities. This change of scale signalled the effective end of the larger gauge railways such as gauge 1

MÄRKLIN STEAM LOCOS AND TANKS
ACCURATELY FINISHED. SUPREME FOR QUALITY, PRICE & EFFICIENCY

IDEAL FOR THE YOUTHFUL ENTHUSIAST

Steam Loco. 2-4-0 Type. Length 13½ ins. Large double-action Cylinders. Safety valve, Steam whistle, etc. Long stroke drive from rear wheel. All four wheels gear-coupled. Gauge 0 (1¼ ins.). Price **37/6**

Type 4-4-2. Length 16½ ins. Fixed double-action cylinders. Automatic reverse or by hand. Safety valve, whistle, fireproof japanning, exhaust pipe in front of engine. Complete accessories, including cylinder oil. N.B.R. colours. Gauge 0 (1¼ ins.) Price **79/6**

Gauge 1 (1¾ ins.) Price **157/-**

Can also be supplied with clockwork mechanism in Gauge 0 at **54/-** Gauge 1 at **95/-**

"FLYING SCOTSMAN"

Gauge 0 (1¼ ins.). Pacific Type 4-6-2. Length 20-ins. Double bogie tender. Fixed double-action cylinders. Reversing gear by hand or automatically operating through stop valve. Safety valve, waste tap, whistle, exhaust pipe, outlet in chimney. Super-heating vaporising spirit lamp. Complete with all accessories, including cylinder oil.
L.N.E.R colouring. Price **130/-**

Gauge 1 (1¾ ins.). Length 25½ ins., with finely registering water and steam gauge. Both the above are magnificent models and rank among the finest produced. Price **168/-**

"LORD NELSON" Type (Southern Railway)

Gauge 1 only. Steam. Loco. 4-6-0 type. Length with double bogie tender 26½ ins. Fixed double-acting cylinders, hand reverse or automatically operating through stop valve. Safety valve, water gauge, steam-pressure gauge, whistle, waste tap, imitation fire box with furnace doors which open. Exhaust-pipe outlet in chimney. Tender contains imitation coal and three oil cylinders. Lockers with hinged lids. Complete with all accessories including cylinder oil. Correct Southern Railway colours. (A prototype of the loco "Lord Nelson.") A magnificent model and a perfect reproduction. Price **168/-**

MÄRKLIN LOCOS
& TRAIN SETS. STEAM & CLOCKWORK
POWERFUL MECHANISM, UNEQUALLED FOR LENGTH OF RUN

STEAM TRAIN SET

Length of train, 40 ins. Engine, Tender and three bogie carriages with doors which open. Loco fitted with brass boiler, fixed single acting cylinders, slip eccentric reversing. Whistle and safety valve. Efficient spirit lamp. Large set oval rails and all accessories. L.M.S. and L.N.E.R. colours. Gauge 0 (1¼ ins.) Price **52/-**
G.W. and S.R. Gauge 1¼. Price **87/-**

STEAM TANK LOCO

STEAM TANK LOCO

(2-axle type.) Length 7¾ ins. Oscillating cylinders, safely valve in fitted cap, whistle. Useful shunting model. L.M.S., L.N.E.R., G.W. and S.R. colours Gauge 0. (1¼ ins.) Price **19/-**

Length 8¾ ins. Fixed single action cylinders. Slip eccentric reversing action. Whistle, safety valve and all accessories. L.M.S., L.N.E.R., G.W. & S.R. colours. Gauge 0. Price **38/-**
L.M.S., L.N.E.R., G.W. Gauge 1. **57/-**

CLOCKWORK TANK LOCO

Reversing gear and speed regulator. Powerful mechanism. Length 9½ ins. L.M.S., L.N.E.R., G.W. & S.R. colours. Gauge 0 Price **42/-**
L.M.S., L.N.E.R., G.W. Gauge 1. **62/-**

CLOCKWORK 6-coupled TANK LOCO

(2-axle type.) Forward and reverse hand or automatic control. Length 6½ ins. L.M.S., L.N.E.R., G.W. and S.R. colours. Made for hard wear. Gauge 0 (1¼ ins.) Price **11/6**

A PERFECT MODEL of the STEPHENSON LOCO

Type 4-6-4. Length 13 in. A splendid reproduction of the Southern Railway's Tank Loco "Stephenson." Automatic braking and reversing, or by hand. A very efficient and well appointed model. Price **57/6**
Gauge 0.
Can also be had in L.M.S. and L.N.E.R. colours without name "Stephenson." Gauge 1. Price **110/-**

Ask for a Copy of the **MARKLIN HANDBOOK** *of "Better Toys"*

HORNBY TRAINS

Gauge O

HORNBY E320 ELECTRIC & No. 3C CLOCKWORK RIVIERA "BLUE" PASSENGER TRAIN SETS

E320 Electric Riviera "Blue" Passenger Train Set

20-VOLT ELECTRIC—AUTOMATIC REVERSING

E320 (20-volt). Locomotive (automatic reversing) with electric headlamp, No. 3 Riviera "Blue" Tender, Riviera "Blue" Dining Car, Riviera "Blue" Sleeping Car, twelve EA2 Curved Rails, four EB1 Straight Rails and a Terminal Connecting Plate. Space required—6ft. 3in. by 4.t. 6in. The Set is supplied in correct Riviera "Blue" Train colours. **Price 67/6**

CLOCKWORK

No. 3C (Clockwork). Locomotive (reversing), No. 3 Riviera "Blue" Tender, Riviera "Blue" Dining Car, Riviera "Blue" Sleeping Car, twelve A2 Curved Rails, three B1 Straight Rails and a BBR1 Straight Brake and Reverse Rail by means of which the Train can be either braked or reversed from the Track. Space required—6ft. 3in. by 4ft. 6in. The Set is supplied in correct Riviera "Blue" Train colours ... ... **Price 55/-**

The components of the above Train Sets are obtainable separately at the following prices :—

Hornby E320 Electric Riviera "Blue" Locomotive (20-volt) automatic reversing (without Tender) ... ... Price 32/6
Hornby No. 3C Clockwork Riviera "Blue" Locomotive, reversing (without Tender) ... ... Price 22/6
Hornby No. 3 Riviera "Blue" Tender Price 5/6 Hornby Riviera "Blue" Dining Car Price 10/6 Hornby Riviera "Blue" Sleeping Car Price 10/6

HORNBY MODELS OF TWO FAMOUS LOCOMOTIVES

HORNBY "SCHOOLS" CLASS LOCOMOTIVE "ETON"

HORNBY 4-6-2 LOCOMOTIVE "PRINCESS ELIZABETH"

This is a fine scale model of the first member of the famous "Schools" class, perhaps the most popular series of locomotives ever produced by the Southern Railway Company. All who are interested in scale-model locomotives, and especially "Southern" enthusiasts, will welcome the "ETON" both for its beauty and its fine performance.

E420 20-volt Electric Automatic Reversing Locomotive. Price **42/-**
No. 4C Clockwork Locomotive. Price **35/-** Tender, Price **6/6**

This is a magnificent scale model of the L.M.S. "Princess Elizabeth" locomotive. It includes all the main features of the actual engine and its finish is of the highest quality. The Hornby 20-volt automatic reversing motor that is fitted ensures abundant power. "Princess Elizabeth" will run on the standard Hornby 2ft. radius track, but to run this fine engine at its highest speed and to show the immense loads it will pull Hornby Solid Steel Track is recommended.

Price, complete with Tender, in special presentation box, **£5 5 0**

The prices of Hornby Rails are given on pages 51/52 (tinplate) and 53 (solid steel). For particulars and prices of Transformers see page 15

27

---

upwards, although obviously there were still many families living in large houses. Indeed, there were many noteworthy garden railways in all scales and gauges at this time, but they tended to be legacies of earlier and more graceful times. Nonetheless, the mass produced electric train was aimed for use in the smaller domestic house. For the first time Britain had an indigenous toy manufacturer who would dominate the popular toy train market for a considerable time. Hornby toy trains were introduced in 1920 as an offshoot of the already established Meccano Company's product range, and in the mid-1920s the original clockwork trains were joined by a range of electric powered types. The principal of these was, in fact, modelled on the electric Metropolitan locomotive, first introduced for the Wembley exhibition of 1925. The first examples were highly dangerous 100 to 250 volt versions and these models were followed by 4 volt and clockwork, then 6 volt and finally 20 volt versions.

Owing to the suspension of German supplies after the First World War, Bassett-Lowke realised its vulnerability and began concentrating on its own manufacture. Its O gauge range was ostensibly to dominate the up-market model train field, whereas Hornby would virtually monopolise the popular toy shop trade.

Above: Hornby's 1937 catalogue offered the Princess Elizabeth *locomotive as the top of their O gauge range and, like the Lionel Hudson (see page 33), it represented the direction in which large-scale manufacturers were heading with steam-outline locomotives prior to their demise in World War II.*

Below: Bassett-Lowke's legendary gauge O Mogul series ran for over 45 years and are a superb tribute to that company's place in the Hall of Fame of the model railway world. Illustrated here is the ubiquitous Stanier Mogul. They were among the first and certainly the last, mass-produced live-steam, gauge O locomotives made entirely in the U.K.

BASSETT-LOWKE LTD

SCALE MODEL

L.M.S. Railway Company's 2-6-0 Type Locomotive. No. 2945.

British Make. **Gauge No. 0.**

29

In Europe Marklin became the most influential force in model trains and their arch rivals, Bing, finally succumbed to the political and economic upheavals of the late 1920s. During this period Marklin produced some of its classic locomotives and indeed, it is arguable that gauge O electric trains reached their zenith in the late 1930s. Though gauge 1 alternatives to most of the gauge O types were available, this relatively large equipment would effectively disappear until some thirty years later when an unexpected revival of that gauge would occur.

The seeds of discussion and argument concerning scale were presaged in 1935 when the National Model Railroad Association (NMRA) determined that gauge O—$\frac{1}{4}$ inch to 1 foot, i.e. $\frac{17}{64}$ of 1 inch to 1 foot equals a scale of 1:48, and therefore deviated from Greenly's accepted European standard of 1:45, which was to be dropped in favour of the NMRA standard.

Several locomotives of this period should be mentioned and ironically the most famous and highly sought after are those made by Marklin for foreign markets. Among them the Swiss Crocodile, the French Mountain Etat and the English Cock O' The North are the most acclaimed. Hornby's gauge O production reached its height with the introduction of the Princess Elizabeth Pacific locomotive in 1937. While mentioning classic O gauge locomotives of this halcyon period, the Lionel Super Hudson of the New York Central Railroad, Class J1E, was an outstanding example. It was built to NMRA standards, although it was also available in coarse scale for use on ordinary Lionel track, and a further high quality scale model, namely a Pennsylvania 0-6-0 class B6 Switcher was also produced by Lionel in a similar form.

Just as the First World War led to the demise of gauge 1, so the Second World War sounded forth the effective death knell of gauge O. It is unlikely that gauge O would have lasted much longer as the predominant commercial gauge, as another development had already dawned in the mid-1930s. It seemed that the quest for more realism, coupled with the ever diminishing amount of space available for play within the house, led to the realisation that even greater reductions would have to take place in model railways if manufacturers were to satisfy the criteria of parents, who after all would, as hitherto, probably make the purchasing decision.

Despite several false dawns, particularly Bing's HO railway (16.5 mm gauge, 3.5 mm to 1 foot) inspired by the collaboration of W. J. Bassett-Lowke with one of the Bing family, the real initiation of HO railways came from the development of Trix railways in Germany. Trix railways were founded by Franz Bing in associa-

Above: It is unlikely that in today's conditions a cigarette manufacturer could advertise in a boys' magazine in this way. It underlines Bassett-Lowke's commercial enterprise in the 1920s when the mass production of a toy locomotive could be offered in this way.

Right: The catalogue cover of one of Bing's last English catalogues, circa 1928.

tion with Stefan Kahn and once again they were encouraged by W. J. Bassett-Lowke. In fact, Trix were to move to England before the outbreak of the Second World War, but from there on much confusion arises as there were two distinct branches of the Trix business, one in England and one in Germany. Relatively new materials were used in the construction of the Trix railway system. Instead of tinplate ballast sections, the track base was made of a black plastic compound into which the three-rail tinplate rails were fixed. One feature was that all the

rails were insulated by the base, thus giving rise to the unique Trix facility for having two or three circuits on one track. The engines were fitted with current pick-up points on either side, that is from each of the outer running rails, and there was, of course, continuous contact with the middle live rail. The wheels were insulated, one from the other, and indeed this was central to the system. The middle rail thus provided the common polarity and the facility to use two or three available circuits. In this way two trains could be run independently of one another at various speeds and in opposite directions. The scale of these early trains was 1:90 and the gauge 16.5 mm. In addition Trix also introduced their own automatic couplings although, of course, Lionel had already adopted a sophisticated automatic coupling for its gauge O equipment, while Marklin and Hornby employed couplings that would join 'automatically' when pushed together. Trix, however, provided for remote-controlled uncoupling. A further innovation for Europe was the construction of the Trix loco bodies from diecastings. The system was operated on 14 volt AC output and the first three locomotive types comprised a four-wheel tender engine, a tank engine and a somewhat shortened Reichsbahn electric type. All the locos had solid diecast wheels with simulated spokes. Vehicles and rolling stock were of traditional lithographed tin plate construction. By late 1937, an excellent representation of a Reichsbahn 03 Pacific was introduced, and it was even more remarkable for the first commercial introduction of a likeness of Walschaert valve gear in this miniature scale. A very attractive diesel was also introduced.

Bassett-Lowke had contracted with Trix to produce British type locomotives to be marketed as Trix Twin around 1935. Among these were the 4-4-0 LMS Deeley Compound type, a Princess Elizabeth Pacific and a Gresley Flying Scotsman type Pacific. A Southern Railway Suburban Motor Unit, using the same powered bogie unit as fitted to the German diesel described earlier, was also available and a unique station-building outfit known as 'The Manyways' system was also introduced. At this early stage HO railways had arrived and over forty years later they continued to form the highest volume selling model railway equipment in the world. Marklin were not aware of these developments, and in 1936 they introduced OO variants of many of their existing O gauge offerings. They adopted a scale of 1:85, but they did not make an attempt to adopt Trix's unique three circuit system. Instead they opted for a relatively simple three-rail system which in one form or another they

L. & N.E.R. (G.N.R. Section)
4-6-2 Pacific Type Locomotive

ELECTRIC.

GAUGE 0 - 1½ ins.
Overall length, 19¼ ins.

THE Locomotive, of which the model illustrated above is a perfect 0 Gauge reproduction, is the " Flying Scotsman," made famous through being exhibited at Wembley, during 1924 and 1925. The original engine, " Great Northern," No. 1470 (now 4470) proved so efficient that many have since been built, slight alterations and modifications having been made to enable these powerful locomotives to run almost anywhere on the now extensive L. & N.E.R. system.

FULL SPECIFICATION.
(This may be simplified to suit Customers).

BODY   Constructed of specially selected materials. Requisite strength has been studied in every way.

MECHANISM   The power unit fitted is specially made for this locomotive. All parts are fitted by hand, thus ensuring perfect running qualities and full power. The electric motor is of permanent magnet type, reversing automatically from the track, and is wound to suit any voltage desired by the purchaser, up to 25 volts.

WHEELS   "Newalloy" or C. I. wheels to order mounted on turned steel axles, running in brass bushes. Bogie has very efficient suspension.

VALVE GEAR   Correct Walschaerts type, exactly as on prototype, and complete in every way. Coupling-rods, connecting rods, eccentric-rods, etc., are fluted.

DETAILS   Practically every external detail on the actual locomotive is included, exactly to scale.

FINISH   The finish of this model is of the highest order. It is enamelled in correct L.N.E.R. colours, and the lining and lettering is executed by hand, great care being taken to ensure correct reduction to scale. Every line on the actual engine is reproduced on the model, including that on the buffer beams, wheel-rims and bosses. Comparison of our illustration with Photographs of No. 4472 will show how perfect this model is. Any name and number may be selected.

Made to order only.

SUPER-DETAIL MODEL.

LO/300 GAUGE 0 Scale, 7 mm. to 1 foot **Price from** £30 0 0 according to Specification.

Cab fittings, from £7 10 0 extra.   **Postage and Packing Free.**

If so desired this model can be supplied with the latest type Corridor Tender.

NOTE.—This locomotive requires a curve of 4 ft. 6 ins. radius in Gauge 0 Larger radii curves are of course advisable where possible.

Above: The Leeds Model Company, formed by R. F. Stedman in the 1920s, continued in business until the early 1960s. Illustrated is their superb gauge O Gresley Pacific in its original form. This particular locomotive was built in very small quantities and was an outstanding model of its time.

Centre right: Edwardian exotica. A PLM Coupe Vent by Schoenner for 3 inch gauge, circa 1903, one of a small range of live steam locomotives put out by this German maker.
Bottom right: Lionel's ultimate gauge O Hudson is now regarded as a supreme collector's piece.

have continued to use until this day. The track was stamped onto a lithographed tinplate ballast base. Marklin even produced a four-wheel simulation of a Commodore Vanderbilt to commence its invasion of the American market. The mid-1930s did not encourage Marklin to produce any English locomotives, although British type coaches in HO by Marklin do exist from this period.

The separation in advertising and promotional literature between OO and HO became a feature in the post Second World War years; the differences are purely that of scale, OO locomotives being slightly larger than their HO equivalents. Therefore, while mechanically they can be run on the same systems, individual items would not match optically. Apart from the liaison with Trix there were no major developments in OO railways in Britain until 1938, although as in so many areas of model railways, small specialised businesses arose to service the needs of the small numbers of dedicated adherents. Stuart Reidpath and later J. S. Beeson and Hamblings became the principal suppliers in this field.

It was about this time that the differences between the continental 3.5 mm to 1 foot HO scale and the essentially English 4 mm to 1 foot OO scale arose. In 1938 Hornby entered the OO field with an excellent range of diecast-bodied trains, including an LNER streamlined Pacific, *Sir Nigel Gresley*, and a 0-6-2 tank engine. Apart from a later conversion to two-rail, these locomotives were available in one form or another right through this system's life until 1964. Thereafter most of the Hornby Dublo locomotive dies were taken over by Wrenn.

America first responded to the challenge of OO railways upon the introduction of the first Bing table railways during the 1920s. As in England no major manufacturer embraced this system initially, but a series of small firms such as Mantua, Varney, Walthers and Scalecraft began to produce components, kits and finished models for this specialised market. This period, namely the late 1920s and early 1930s, saw the real birth of the kit business. The Americans adopted the 3.5 scale and therefore their products have always been compatible with their European cousins. The first mass marketing of small gauge railways was taken up by Knapp, and these products, while excellent, were regrettably to coincide with the outbreak of the Second World War. American Flyer in 1938 also produced diecast HO derivatives among others of their O gauge Hudson, but these locomotive HO products were not reintroduced until the end of the 1950s. Lionel produced one of the most interesting small scale railways, but decided to use the OO scale while employing a 19-mm gauge track. A Hudson locomotive for two- or three- rails was available with a range of several freight cars, but this was not to reappear after World War II, although Lionel later became involved with conventional HO railways.

When the manufacturers were able to recommence production after the Second World War, O gauge became relegated to a minor part of their programmes and every effort was given over to the re-establishment of the model train enthusiast market and the encouragement of conversion to HO/OO scale. Hornby Dublo in England resumed marketing when supplies were available once again after 1947 and in the early 1950s they were challenged by Tri-ang, who started with an all plastic railway system which was not only cheaper than Hornby's but also had the very real attraction of two-rail operation with its more realistic trackwork. Attempts to reduce scale and gauge even further came to little and Tri-ang

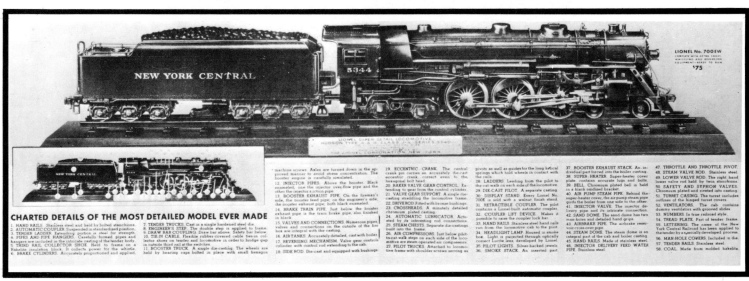

CHARTED DETAILS OF THE MOST DETAILED MODEL EVER MADE

Extreme left top: Latterday Hornby — a model of an LMS Duchess Class Pacific *by Hornby Dublo, the final version of Hornby trains.*

Centre left top: German HO — A Fleischmann layout shown at the Model Railway Exhibition Central Hall, London. This layout took six months to build and was based on a design from the German magazine Kurier.

Left: A continental village is brought to mind by this group of model buildings built by Faller.

Below: Trix model of No 4472 Flying Scotsman *in 4 mm scale.*

A craftsman with over 50 years service at the legendary works of Bassett-Lowke Limited in Northampton is here seen assembling the last batch of gauge O live steam Stannier Moguls in 1969.

with its TT3 range (scale 1:102) and Wesa and Zueke on the continent with their TT scale (1:120) achieved little success. An associated company of Bassett-Lowke's, namely Winteringham Limited, were virtually bankrupted by their unsuccessful attempt to mass produce Trix Twin railways in England — German expertise does not always travel! Marklin continued its three-rail AC system, while virtually every other manufacturer in Europe and America adopted a two-rail, 12 volt DC arrangement. Fleischmann, Liliput and Riverossi — first in diecast, then in injection moulded plastic — rose to great peaks of perfection in the manufacture of highly detailed equipment. Joueff of France, and Lima of Italy also became major producers, initially

at the lower end of the market.

Although America at this time had an indigenous model train manufacturing industry, the business polarised in the post-war years in that HO scale model railways moved away from the traditional toy shop image. This was achieved historically through America's fashioning of Japanese manufacturing techniques, and as the years rolled by, vast orders for Japanese-produced lost wax, brass cast locomotives flowed into Japan. During the 1950s and early 1960s standards that were almost undreamed of for small scale, batch-produced models were achieved and even O gauge derivatives manufactured in this way achieved an excellence that could hardly be bettered by the one-off model. With certain excep-

tions, the standards achieved by the American/Japanese collaboration in model railways has not been bettered since, although one is bound to say that this was restricted almost entirely to locomotives with only a few pieces of rolling stock being manufactured in this way. In the post-war years it is fair to say that the American market was by far and away the most sophisticated and discerning in the way that it demanded high standards that were by no means universally sought in Europe. The continental manufacturers tended to specialise in ready-to-run, fully automated systems with great emphasis placed on automatic operation, points accessories and train running incorporating very sophisticated isolating procedures for starting and stopping.

In England the development was a mixture of ready-to-run in its own isolated 4 mm scale and white metal kits etc, and it was probably the lack of export potential to America which led to a gradual decline in standards, when compared with their European and Japanese competitors. For the serious modeller, the growth of white metal kits became the alternative to the pronounced lack of advanced scale locomotives sold in a ready-to-run state at a price the average customer could afford. All this time saw the tremendous growth in the interest in collecting vintage model and toy trains, and it was partially as a result of this movement that several major manufacturers re-introduced mass-produced plastic O gauge in the late 1960s. The amount of detail that could be achieved with sophisticated plastic injection techniques far outweighed anything that was possible in the vintage pre-war years. For all this, however, it was very difficult for plastic to recreate the characteristic 'clank' of the tinplate train and whereas several firms such as Lima in Italy still produce fairly extensive ranges of O gauge equipment, they do not mount a serious challenge to HO. An even more remarkable return to old times was Marklin's decision to re-introduce gauge 1, but this time it was to be a two-rail system. An excellent diesel and steam outline locomotive in finely moulded plastic came on the market in 1970. It is generally conceded that a system that cannot be rapidly expanded will not succeed in the cut and thrust of the market place. Whether poor initial sales

Above: Japanese genius. Japanese model train makers were to achieve unparalleled excellence in the manufacture of metal model locomotives in the post-war period. This excellence was based mainly on their unrivalled application of the lost wax casting system, and the Big Boy pictured here in O gauge typifies the standards achieved in the 1950s and 1960s. Giving the Big Boy scale is another Japanese brass locomotive supplied by Westside for HOn3 scale in America. The wooden cars are typical of the many excellent kit-made items made available to the American market.

Below: The beginnings of OO gauge. Although at least a decade before its time, Bing, in association with Bassett-Lowke, produced an extensive tinplate OO railway system in the 1920s both in clockwork and, less successfully, three-rail electric. Curiously enough, when Hornby marketed their 'Dublo' system in 1938, they too offered a clockwork alternative, although this form of propulsion was discontinued by virtually all the OO and HO manufacturers after World War II.

determined Marklin's decision to keep the range relatively small or for whatever other reasons, the system is now virtually obsolete.

One of the big success stories in the return to large scale mass production of model railways was in Lehmann's Gross Bahn (LGB) system introduced in 1968. This was basically a narrow gauge system which was suitable for operating indoors or in the garden. Although running on gauge 1 track, the locomotives and rolling stock were, of course, built to a much larger scale, roughly equivalent to the old gauge 3, 1:23 scale. These immensely robust trains, unlike anything else on the market, could be used by child and adult alike. Several other more specialised firms produced O and 1 gauge items in relatively limited runs, directly aimed at the collectors' market. One of the first in this field was Wilag, in association with Fulgurex in Switzerland, with a splendid Maffei Pacific in gauge 1 for steam (butane gas fired) or electric together with a really superb range of continental outline cars which were initially accurate replicas of Marklin's extremely rare 57 mm pre-war cars. Later the range of Wilag cars was extended to become a series

Above: Gauge 1 — A Bing for Bassett-Lowke model of a Great Northern Railway 4-4-2 on the layout of J. Francis Parker.

Right: A 4 mm Scale, Gauge 16.5 mm is shown on the Reverend Teddy Boston's layout based on Great Western Railway practice.

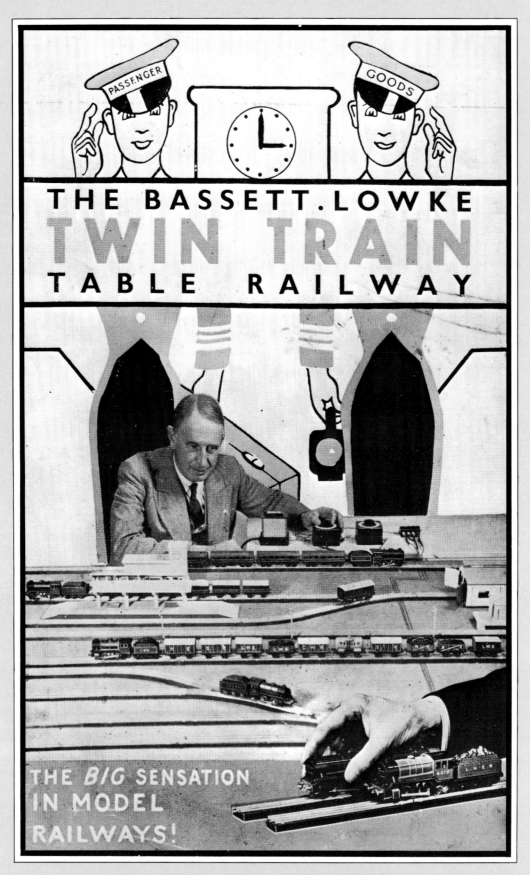

Above: W. J. Bassett-Lowke plays trains
with one of the products of his association
with the German Trix company in the
mid-1930s. From the introduction of the
legendary Black Prince locomotives in
1901 to the cessation of Bassett-Lowke's
models in the 1960s, his imprint on the
world of model trains was unsurpassed.

Right and below: Trix Twin, founded by a member of the Bing family, was the first complete HO electric model railway system marketed. Illustrated here are two presentation sets of the late 1930s. All pre-war Trix Twin equipment is highly sought after by collectors.

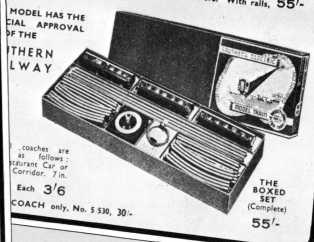
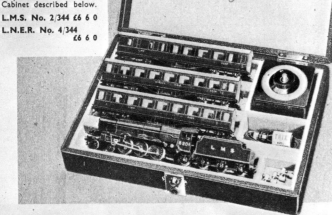

*Left: 3.5 mm Scale. Gauge 16.5 mm –
John B. Porter's HO scale American
layout with Canadian connections. A
well-weathered CNR 2-8-0.is on the
turntable outside the roundhouse.*

Separate items

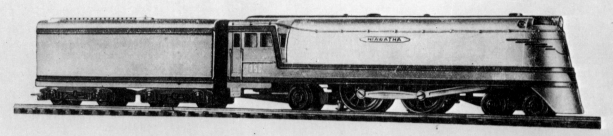

L 442/R [3-15-0]

All locomotives in the red line, are supplied exclusively to operate on 4,5-12 volts D.C. two rail track.

For the same locomotive but operating on A.C. 16 volts see our BLUE catalogue.

Streamlined locomotive « Atlantic » type with tender, in all details reproducing the American « Milwaukee Road », with the following main features: remote control reversing - automatic coupling - insulated wheels - very powerful motor with worm wheel transmission in an oil bath - continuous lubrification of the bearings. Supplied in black or dark green or silver and orange.
Length with tender: 33 cms. Supplied in red box of 35 x 6 x 5 cms. - weight 950 gr.

Complete view of main frame with motor and transmission (without balancing weights).

All our locomotives have insulated wheels in order to be aBle to operate them on two rail track.

Tri-ang RAILWAYS LOCOMOTIVES

OO HO GAUGE

R.251   0–6–0 Class 3F Tender Loco. .. **32/6**
R.33   Tender for R.251.   ..   .. **5/3**

R.258   4–6–2 "The Princess Royal" Loco—maroon livery, with Walschaerts Gear. **54/-**
R.34   Tender for R.258. ..   ..   .. **6/7**

R.253   0–4–0 Dock Shunter, with working headlight. **31/6**

R.55   B–B Diesel Loco, with working headlight. **57/9**
R.57   B–B Diesel Loco—non-powered. **17/6**
R.58   Diesel " B " Unit—non-powered. **15/9**

R.155   Diesel Switcher, with working headlights. **56/-**

44

in its own right. Hosts of small manufacturers, mainly in Germany, produced all-metal O gauge railway equipment which equalled the best of the American/Japanese equipment referred to earlier, but they were considerably more expensive. Finally, in 1976 a Japanese typewriter manufacturer, Astor, produced a magnificent live steam gauge 1 Schools class locomotive which for all the world reflected how Bing might have made gauge 1 locomotives had the firm survived to the 1970s. Following the success of this first locomotive, Astor went on to produce an early 4-4-0 American type and a Japanese 0-6-0 tender locomotive. More recently they produced an extraordinary Shay narrow gauge type, a PLM Pacific, for gauge 1 in live steam. Perhaps their entry into the market was timed to reflect the fact that some early vintage toy trains had reached such astronomic price levels. Probably they felt that the time had come to play live-steam trains again, but this time they had no illusions about the market they were aiming for, and they recognised that their customers would be well attuned to the models being priced in the region of £500 to £600 without any undue alarm.

The only major threat to the supremacy

Top left: In the early post-war years, Rivarossi of Italy was among the first European manufacturers to market ready-to-run HO equipment for the American market. This relatively crude Milwaukee Road Atlantic illustrates Rivarossi's unique flexible drive system.

Bottom left: A page from a Tri-ang catalogue showing British and export models — the latter were short-lived.

Bottom right: A superb Japanese-produced, lost-wax, brass-cast model by Tenshodo.

of HO/OO model railways was in the perfection of small scale electric motors which could be fitted to N gauge locomotives. N gauge uses a 9 mm track, and once again European manufacturers dominated the world scene. The historical development of N gauge, which is roughly half the size of OO, started in the late 1950s with non-motorised treble O diecast locomotives and rolling stock put out by Lone Star in Britain. These were merely pushed along pre-formed sections of cast track. In 1959 the N system was motorised to run on two-rail plastic track. Arnold Rapido in Germany next produced a similar scale electric train system using the same 9 mm gauge. The scale was, at this time 1:152, but this was soon to be changed to the more accurate scale of 1:160. Minitrix were next in the field, to be followed by Fleischmann and Rivarossi. Marklin continued their highly individual approach and even introduced a 6.5 mm gauge railway known as Z gauge, but it suffered from the disadvantage that it was not interchangeable with any other system and therefore its long term appeal was limited. The big selling point of N gauge is, of course, the fact that a fairly complicated system can be built in an even

R.152   0-6-0   Diesel   Shunter—
green livery. **35/-**

R.59   2-6-2   Class 3MT   Tank Loco.   **52/6**

R.54   4-6-2 " Pacific " Loco, with working headlight.
   54/-
R.32   Tender for R.54.   ..   ..   **6/7**

Narrow Gauge: N gauge OO/9 scale layout belonging to David and Robin Edwards.

| AFM/R | without headlight | 114/6d |
| AFM/R | with headlight | 128/6d |

| ANI/R | with lights | 126/-d |
| ANI/T | trailer coach | 43/9d |

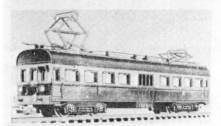

| A2002/R | with lights | 147/-d |
| V2002 | trailer coach | 43/9d |

| Le 626/V | with lights | 99/9d |
| Le 424/R | with lights | 155/2d |

| L B & O/V | with headlight | 70/-d |
| L 442/R | Crusader with headlight | 176/2d |

RIVAROSSI locomotives are particularly suitable for running on Hornby-Dublo track. They can be supplied already fitted with centre collectors and Dublo type couplings ready to roll. Take advantage now of adding that extra locomotive to your collection.

CONVERSION PRICES
Conversion with Rivarossi couplings	12/6d
Conversion with one Dublo type coupling	15/-d
Conversion with two Dublo type couplings	17/6d

SM FM	...	...	...	...	...	95/4d
SM A2002	...	...	...	...	...	109/8d
SM ANI	...	...	...	...	...	86/4d
SM B & O	...	...	...	...	...	67/4d
SM 442	...	...	...	...	...	141/9d
SM 626	...	...	...	...	...	96/10d
SM 424	...	...	...	...	...	122/6d

RIVAROSSI loco kits are something different. Packed in smart display boxes, they contain every single part required to build a particular locomotive. Comprehensive instructions with an exploded view diagram are included with every kit. Construction is simple if you follow the instructions, and when finished, you have a model you can really be proud of.

| L 221/R | with headlight | 186/8d |
| L SP/R | with headlight | 186/8d |

L SP/R is illustrated on front cover.

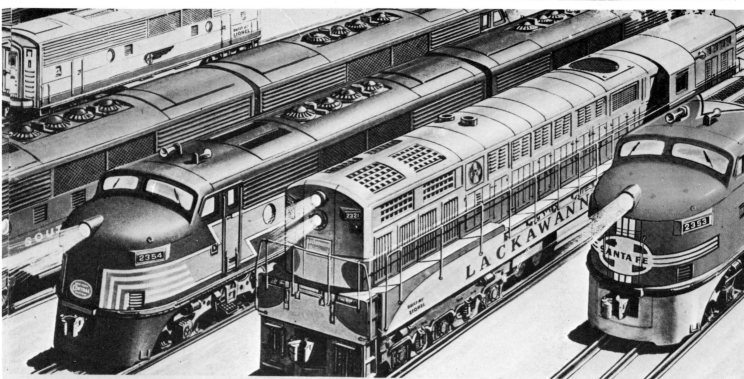

Lionel 'O' Diesels with Magne-Traction

No. 2356 SOUTHERN RAILWAYS TWIN-UNIT DIESEL—Take a look at Southern's great green twin-unit Diesel — equipped with two worm-drive motors, built-in horn and *MAGNE-TRACTION.* It consists of two GM-type "A" units — has headlights and remote control operating knuckle couplers on both ends. Overall length 26½". **$47.50**

No. 2354 NEW YORK CENTRAL TWIN DIESEL — Pride of the New York Central — these big twin GM "A" units. Lionel model counterparts have two worm-drive motors in the forward unit. They're equipped with built-in horn and *MAGNE-TRACTION.* Overall length of both units is 26½". **$47.50**

No. 2321 FAIRBANKS-MORSE DIESEL — Brand new Diesel type. Modelled after the Fairbanks-Morse loco built for the Lackawanna R.R. Has two worm-drive motors, *MAGNE-TRACTION* and built-in horn. Head end is completely illuminated, including headlight, Mars light, classification lights and markers. This Diesel is 17" long. **$43.50**

No. 2353 SANTA FE TWIN-UNIT DIESEL — Everybody is familiar with this Santa Fe powerhouse — it pulls the Emperor Chief. Like all these big Lionel GM double "A" units it is equipped with two worm-drive motors, built-in horn and *MAGNE-TRACTION.* Length 26½". Has headlights and operating knuckle couplers on both pilot ends. **$47.50**

"B" UNITS FOR GM-TYPE DIESELS—This year Lionel makes available three Diesel "B" units to match the double "A's" shown above. They're blueprint-accurate in design — measure more than 13 inches long. Used between your big "A" units they'll make an engine nearly 40" long.

No. 2343C SANTA FE	
No. 2344C NEW YORK CENTRAL	Each $9.95
No. 2356C SOUTHERN RAILWAYS	

31

Lokomotiven

104
Bauzug-Diesellokomotive, Achsfolge B, mit Sitzbänken für die Streckenarbeiter, Kompressorkessel und Arbeitsscheinwerfer. Im Einsatz für den Streckendienst und Gleisbau der Bahnmeistereien.
Länge über Puffer 45 mm.

105
Nebenbahn-Dampflokomotive, Achsfolge B, Tenderlokomotive mit Rauchfang, Kurbelstangen und Kreuzkopf naturgetreu bewegt. Vor allem für den schweren Güter- und Personenzugdienst auf Nebenbahnstrecken geeignet.
Länge über Puffer 49 mm.

106
Lokalbahn-Dampflokomotive „Feuriger Elias", Achsfolge B, Originalnachbildung der Oberrheinischen Eisenbahngesellschaft (OEG). Diese verkleidete Straßen-Lokomotive wird zum Teil heute noch für den Personen- und Güterzugdienst auf Nebenbahnstrecken eingesetzt. Länge über Puffer 51 mm.

**hochübersetztes Schneckengetriebe für naturgetreue Langsamfahrt ● Allradantrieb
fernsteuerbar für Vor- und Rückwärtsfahrt ● Kupplungshaken an beiden Enden**

EGGER-BAHN

Top left: Rivarossi catalogue with page showing continental and American prototypes but with text emphasizing their suitability for running on Hornby Dublo track.

Bottom left: Lionel was one of the few major manufacturers to successsfully market gauge O equipment for the mass market in the post-war years. Their main rivals in Europe, namely Marklin and Hornby, had virtually discontinued serious manufacture of gauge O trains at this time. Perhaps the popularity of diesel types in America and the suitability of modelling them in injection moulded plastic was one of the main reasons for this trend. Lionel's post-war, steam outline locomotives offered little in terms of appearance and were toy-like in an age which had come to expect accurate scale appearance in its locomotives.

smaller space than its HO counterpart. Aspects of this are discussed in later chapters.

An interesting historical footnote is that Bing produced a beautifully lithographed tinplate set around 1910 which demonstrated that the techniques for building sub-miniature scale trains existed at that time, but there is little evidence to suggest that the market was anywhere near ready to accept this degree of miniaturisation in these early days of the hobby.

Our survey of the growth and development of the model train concludes with the thought that although the steam locomotive has disappeared as a major source of motive power over most of the globe, more models of steam locomotives are sold than those of their modern successors, the diesels and the electric locomotives. Perhaps one of the other secrets of the model train is that it enables earlier times and memories to be kept alive while the real world races on. As a final tribute to the world's love affair with the steam locomotive, George Stephenson's famous *Rocket* is being offered as a live-steam HO model (Swiss made) and in $3\frac{1}{2}$ inch gauge by Hornby.

Above: Egger-Bahn was one of the first manufacturers to introduce N gauge trains of scale appearance in the 1960s, although they were larger than their successors as this firm decided to model narrow-gauge stock to run on N gauge track (see tables). Although they enjoyed limited success Egger-Bahn went out of business in the late 1960s.

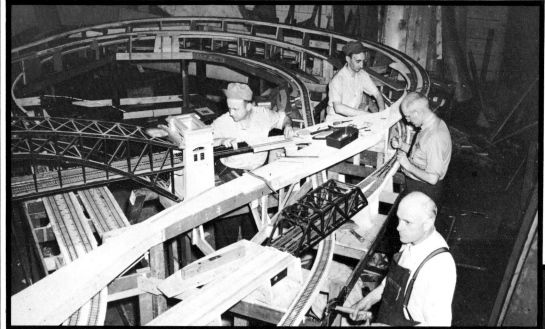

American Railroading in the 1940s

The significant aspect of these models is that they were all made and assembled prior to the era of the state of art which brought us lost-wax-castings, plastic components and the great brass deluge from Japan. Further, there is only one photo in HO scale, all others are in O scale (1:48 — $\frac{1}{4}$ inch scale).

The Detroit Model Railroad Club presents a few club layout building scenes and subsequent operating scenes. The art of constructing first-class club layouts was developed to a fine degree in the USA. These pictures were taken in 1940–42.

Above: Typical construction and foundation work of an O scale layout

Right centre: Switchwork and track-laying operations. The switches are pre-assembled in fixtures and then spiked in position on the layout — intermediate rail-work is completed later.

Top right: After trackwork is complete, scenery components are pre-assembled on the bench and installed on the layout.

Bottom right: Operating practice is a relief from the tedium of building and wiring a layout and the beginning of advance scheduled model operating practices.

Extreme right centre: An operating interlock tower (as with actual railroad practice) is but one of many technical and mechanical achievements reproduced for the pleasure of playing trains.

Above left: This ¼-inch scale model of Pegasus was modelled on the first horizontal boiler steam locomotives built for the Baltimore & Ohio Railroad. It was built by Mel Thornburgh and was shown on a travelling exhibition layout sponsored by the Baltimore & Ohio RR.

Above right: A partially completed model of a Lehigh Valley Camelback Atlantic-type locomotive is track-tested on the layout.

Right: A model of the General of Civil War fame pulls a pair of old-time coaches through a Howe Truss bridge. The General was built by Jack Ferris who had a model locomotive works in Huntington, Indiana and who built custom railroad models – this one for Kirke Comstock of Albion, Michigan. It is two-rail ¼-inch scale. The two passenger cars were of balsa-wood construction. Kirk Ferris built the combine from kits prepared by the Hawk Model Airplane Company. The Howe Truss bridge was constructed from a kit prepared by Scale Structures Company of California and it had nut bolt castings, threaded tension rods, milled timber and many other small castings. The coach was built by Emery J. Gulash.

Extreme left, top: This model was of the Thatcher Perkins Class. It was a ten-wheeler designed for passenger service and an improvement over the similar wheel arrangement used on the Winans Camel type.

Centre top: A typical American ten-wheeler and train.

Below: This model was also a Ross Winans design and was described as a Camel type. They were used for freight service.

Left: One of the Detroit Model Railroad Club members, Kirke Comstock, was an avid model locomotive collector and in 1942 he had undoubtedly, the largest collection of ¼-inch scale models in the USA. This gauge O ¼-inch scale model of Western & Atlanta Railroad's *General* was built by Scale Model Railway.

Below: A Flint Père Marquette ¼-inch scale Mogul model built by Scale Model Railway. DC or permanent magnet motors were not available for O scale models when this model was built, so AC motors were used with a rectifier to permit DC operations. The reverse switch was connected to the rod sticking out behind the front driver.

Above: Indiana Harbor Belt 0-8-0 switcher built by Scale Model Railway for Kirke Comstock ($\frac{1}{4}$-inch scale, two rail operation). The motor was an AC type with a DC rectifier in the tender to permit two rail operation with reverse control. It was built about 1939.

Below: Bill Lenoir's Chicago Great Western No 355 2-8-0 Consolidation.

Above: Bill Lenoir's CGW No 507 4-6-0 ten-wheeler.

Left: Bill Lenoir's CGW No 116 Mogul 2-6-0.

Below: Bill Lenoir's CGW No 930 4-6-2 Pacific type.

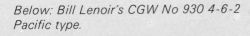

Top left: Just after World War II there was another locomotive manufacturer called Great Western Locomotive Works, who produced a 2-6-0 Mogul gauge O ¼-inch scale. This is a free-lance model with plain castings and somewhat crude.

Above: The Great Western models also had an HO model of a 2-8-0 Consolidation called the Brass Betsy.

Top centre and right: Emery J. Gulash built these two old-time freight car models. Plans were derived from old car builder's encyclopedias. He built the NYC & HR box car and coke car from scratch materials. The box car has strathmore board (paper) sides but all other details are brass and wire stock. The coke car is from wood strip stock; both models are hand lettered.
Top centre: NYC & HR 36 foot box car O gauge ¼-inch scale.
Top right: NYC & HR coke car O gauge ¼-inch scale.

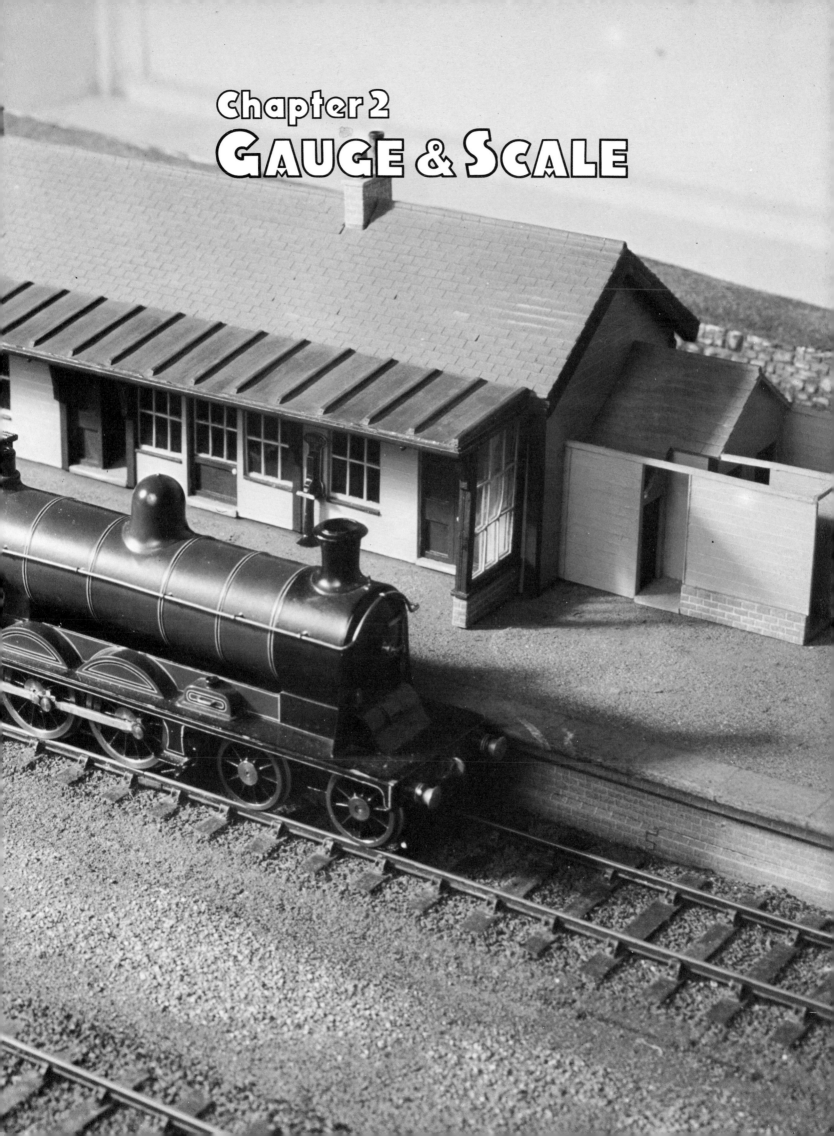

Chapter 2
GAUGE & SCALE

Gauge and scale are often confused when describing model railway equipment. Confusion arises principally because unlike other model forms where the only reduction from the real object may be measured as a simple fraction, i.e. 1/32nd scale or 1/72nd scale=1 inch of model to, say 32 or 72 inches of real aircraft, car etc, model railways have two dimensions to scale down.

The problem with model trains is that not only is one reducing the size of the hardware, e.g. locomotives, rolling stock, signals, etc, but also the width of track on which they run and to which they relate. It is generally agreed that reasonably accurate scaling down of locomotives is possible, but no such consensus exists when it comes to the exact scaling down of rail section and back-to-back measurements of wheels. (See diagram).

For the vast majority of model rail enthusiasts, the quest for the ultimate truth in scale is not an all-consuming passion. If the model train layout gives the impression or illusion of looking 'right' then this will usually suffice. It is arguable that some of the most primitive and extremely coarse scale commercial railway systems conveyed a greater feeling of the reality of a 'proper' railway, because they provided that extra dimension of noise and weight. These are vital ingredients in the creation of illusion and they defy any attempt, even by the purist, to reduce them to 'scale' with any accuracy. The clatter of vintage Lionel, Hornby or Marklin trains is a feature that is immensely difficult to recreate by simply reducing the measurements with clinical mathematical accuracy.

Now let us have a brief look at the measurements of scale and gauge. Remember, scale is the measurement of the reduction from the original, sometimes expressed as a fraction. Gauge is the measurement of the distance between the rails, and this is normally expressed as a symbol, i.e. O, I, HO, N etc. The reason for this probably stems from the fact that standard gauge, i.e. 4 feet 8½ inches, while in widespread use, is by no means operated universally, but the expression O gauge (the first truly popular commercial model gauge) is universally accepted as denoting 1¼ inches between the rails. The fact that a gauge is a known distance between the rails does not presume that the equipment designed to run on these tracks is necessarily of the same scale — HO and OO railways run on an identical gauge, 16.5 mm, but the equipment is built to 4 mm and 3.5 mm to the foot respectively.

The principal gauges adopted by the commercial manufacturers over the years are as follows, and for this purpose they are grouped under two broad categories, Europe and North America:

Above: An LMS Stanier Class 5 4-6-0 constructed when the builder was still at school, on Bob Ledger's stud contact O gauge layout.

Right: Wakefield Model Railway Society's 4 mm scale layout based on LMS (Midland Section) practice. This general view of a goods yard shows the effect of large radius sweeping curves.

Below: A North Eastern Railway coal wagon on Bill Tate's 7 mm coarse scale model railway.

EUROPE
Gauge 4
Gauge 3
Gauge 2
Gauge 1
Gauge O
Gauge HO
Gauge OO
Gauge TT
Gauge N

Specialist gauges and scales include those adopted by the advanced modellers and supported by various specialist manufacturers:

Gauge 1 – Fine Scale
Gauge O – Fine Scale
EEM and EM

NORTH AMERICA
Standard Gauge
1 Gauge
O Gauge
S Gauge
HO Gauge
N Gauge

There are, of course, those modellers who prefer to scale down narrow-gauge railway equipment rather than adhering to these broad categories. This normally results in much larger scale locomotives, etc, running on track made for smaller equipment. Therefore, a narrow-gauge locomotive built to a scale of 7 mm to the foot, i.e. that which would normally

Left: A Tri-ang B12/2 4-6-0 passes a Hornby Dublo (three rail) Stanier 8F 2-8-0. An effective scene showing excellent use of proprietary items on Brian Lunn's British Railway's system.

Above: A close-up of the goods yard. The goods stock is a mixture of Hornby Dublo, Airfix and scratch built. Brian Lunn's system is 4 mm scale 16 mm gauge and uses Peco streamline track.

run on O gauge track, would in narrow gauge modelling ride on HO track. A list of the principal narrow gauge designations is given below:

Gm Narrow Gauge for Gauge 1
On
On3
On2
HOn3
OOn3

For fuller details of Gauge and Scale see table page 86/87. The diagram below gives a good indication of the relative sizes of three of the more popular scales and gauges and, of course, the modeller's choice of gauge will principally be determined by available space. Aspects of this will be dealt with in the chapter on planning the layout. It should be stressed, however, that the other major factor in planning the railway, the cost, does not necessarily reduce in proportion to the scale or gauge as, apart from the individual cost of particular items of railway equipment, there is a tendency for modellers in the smaller scale to buy more equipment than their counterparts

Above: Motive power depot – Marthwaite second version 1965–67 on the 4 mm scale EM gauge constructed by David Jenkinson.

Below: HO gauge 3.5 mm scale is standard for both the European Continent and the USA. This realistic scene shows Mulbach Station on the Continental layout of Alan Spetch.

modelling in the larger scales. As a general guide, however, an N gauge locomotive, which is approximately half the size of its HO counterpart is certainly not half its price and in many cases may be more expensive than a similar model in a much larger scale.

Let us now consider the most popular and widely used gauges today.
O gauge: Although gauge 1 and some gauge 1 derivatives, namely the LGB narrow gauge system discussed earlier, have enjoyed some revival in recent years there is little doubt that the most popular large gauge for which a reasonable amount of proprietary equipment is available is O gauge. This is unmistakably the largest size of the three most popular gauges we will discuss here, namely O gauge, HO/OO gauge and N gauge. The distance between the tracks is $1\frac{1}{4}$ inches and the principal advantage of O gauge equipment is that it is rugged and able to withstand far greater rough handling and maltreatment than its small gauge counterparts. A steam outline O gauge locomotive will measure some 15 inches and weigh between three and

Left: Gardeners pause to watch LMS Jubilee Class 4-6-0 No 5573 Newfoundland *pass Holbeck shed with a Leeds to Glasgow Express on the 4 mm scale layout of the Wakefield Model Railway Society.*

Left: Proprietary produced Continental models, outside the locomotive shed on the German HO scale layout of Alan Spetch.

Left: Haddon (low level) station on The 2 mm Scale Association, Midland group's exhibition layout.

A locomotive shed with Hornby Dublo and Tri-ang locomotives plus a Fowler 0-8-0 made from a Cotswold kit with a K's motor.

four pounds. Although one can run an O gauge train in a circle 27 to 30 inches in diameter, it is when one comes to expand the system that problems arise. O gauge is more suited to the permanent layout and as such will probably require its own room. Principal manufacturers of O gauge equipment today are Lionel in the United States, Lima and Rivarossi in Italy. The latter firms make a full range of international equipment, including European and American types.

HO/OO gauge: This gauge is undoubtedly the most popular miniature gauge manufactured today. The gauge between the rails is $\frac{5}{8}$ inch. A typical steam outline locomotive will measure about 7 to 9 inches and weigh around one pound. An elaborate layout can be built in an area of, say, 6 feet by 9 feet, and an attractive branch line system in even less space. The range of equipment is enormous and the more popular manufacturers are Tyko in the United States and in Europe Marklin, Fleischmann, Hornby, Pallitoy, Wrenn, Airfix and Graham Farish.

N gauge: The perfection of small scale electric motors over the last decade has led to the rapid increase in popularity of this truly sub-miniature railroad system. N gauge is approximately half the size of HO and probably represents the final practical miniature scale. The one obvious advantage is that fairly complex

Right, top and bottom: A 3.5 mm scale HO gauge American prototype model railway in Curacao belonging to Mr and Mrs Nixon. To give some idea of the work behind this magnificent scenic layout the following statistics are very relevant. The layout has: 6000 trees, 600 buildings, 350 road vehicles, 2000 lights, 125 points, 3000 feet of track, 12,000 feet of wire, 425 coaches, 6 multiple-unit trains, 14 steam engines, 1500 wagons/cars, and so on.

Below: Rio Grande in Miniature. *Cliff Young's HO gauge 3.5 mm scale model of 50 miles of the Rio Grande's track from Denver to the Moffat Tunnel in a spiral consists of three circuits of a room 21' 0" × 8' 6". Below is Denver Union Station with a California Zephyr ready to leave. On the top track Akane 2-8-2 No 1213 climbs with a freight train to Pine Cliff.*

layouts can be incorporated in relatively small spaces. As has been mentioned earlier this does not necessarily allow the cost factor to reduce proportionately. For more practical purposes virtually all modern proprietary systems, particularly N gauge, are two-rail; a notable exception is the long-established firm of Marklin in Germany, who still actively market a three-rail system using a centre stud pick-up for the current. Handling N gauge equipment of course entails far greater care and factors such as dust on the track can cause far more problems in smooth running than on the more robust HO and O gauge systems.

Given that all the systems discussed and marketed today are almost exclusively run by electricity, it would be as well now to examine some of the basic principles of how an electric railway system works. Small scale electric trains can, of course, be operated by battery (as discussed earlier) and this is undoubtedly the exception rather than the rule. The vast majority of model railways are operated via transformers direct from the mains. Mains current is usually 110 volts AC or 240 volts DC and, of course, delivering a current of this strength direct to the track would be exceedingly dangerous. Therefore this current has to be stepped down and in most instances it is reduced to 12 volts DC. This reduction in voltage is accomplished through a transformer, which today is normally incorporated in the power pack which will also determine the degree of power delivered to the tracks and thereby the speed of the trains. For AC systems, a rectifier is necessary to convert the current from AC to DC. In these instances the wiring instructions on the power pack are usually perfectly clear but one must be quite careful to make sure that the direct current to the tracks is wired to the appropriate terminals. Power packs sometimes have split outputs: that is, accessories are often worked off alternating current (AC), whereas the trains are almost invariably worked off direct current (DC). Assuming that the original layout commenced from a train set, then the method of attaching the two wires from the power pack to the track will have already been incorporated in a terminal track which will have two screws or clips to receive the terminals from the power pack. Once the current is turned on from the mains the power is delivered through the track, thence to the locomotive wheels which are insulated one from the other. Thus the power is directed to the motor and then to complete the circuit, it flows through the opposite wheels, back through the track and back to the power pack. With the older systems, the centre rail was the live rail through which current was delivered to the motor via a pick-up underneath

Below: A 4 mm scale LNWR Prince of Wales *Class 4-6-0 built to EM gauge by Mr Richards. The motor in the tender is a Zenith with a flywheel fixed to the armature shaft for slow running. The motor is connected to the driving wheels by means of gears and a flexible shaft.*

Left: Steam in the 1930s. *The ever-present lure of steam was catered for by Bowman Models of Dereham, Norfolk. This enterprising firm produced a wide range of stationary engines, steam launches plus their O gauge locomotives of which the best known was the 4-4-0 No 234. This engine was proudly advertised as being of Gauge 1 proportions but running on Gauge O track! Technically it was an oscillating cylinder 4-2-2-0 and it ran for 40 minutes at a filling — one of Bowman's selling points. This rare Bowman coloured advertisement commemorates No 234's achievements at the British Industries Fair when it pulled six large coaches over 183 miles during the week of the show.*

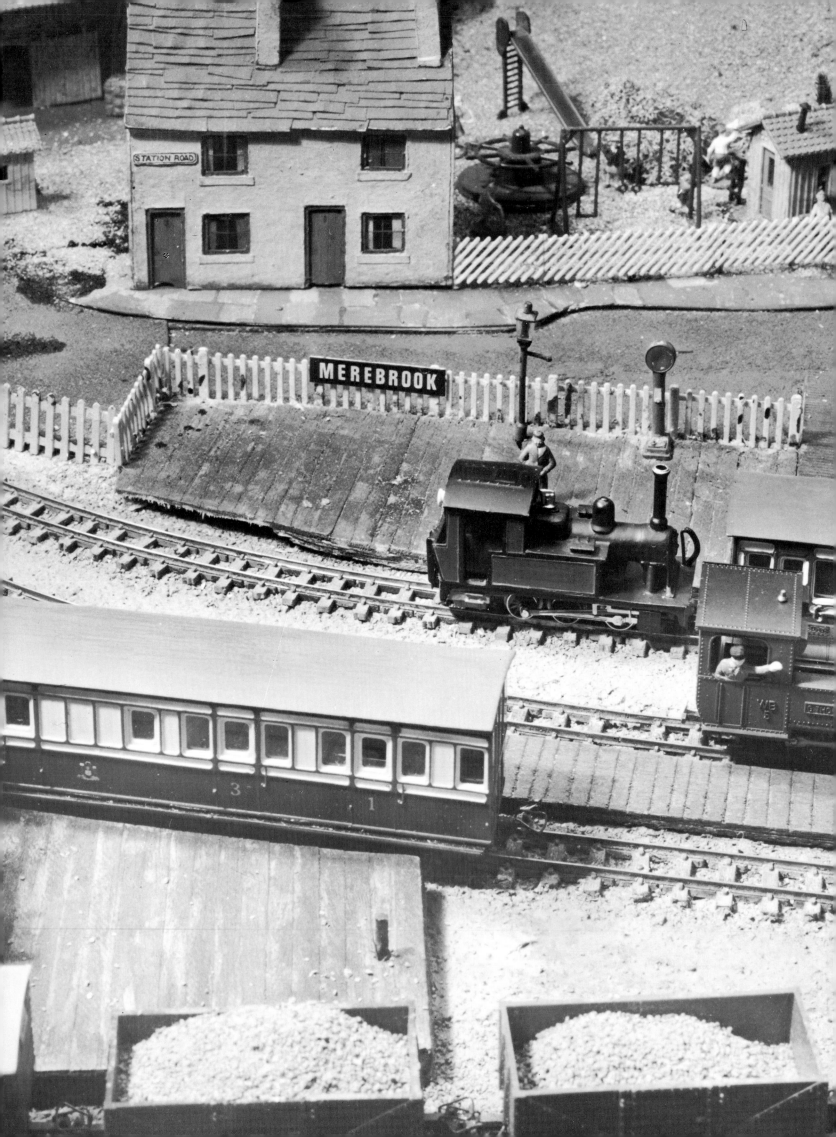

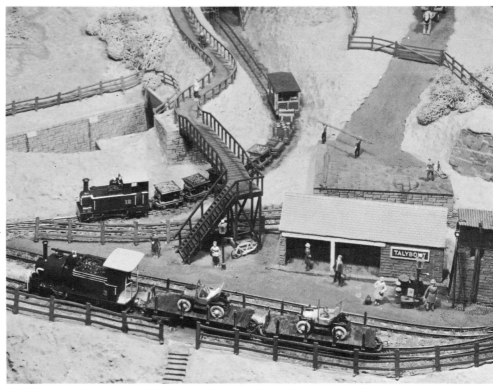

Top: A proprietary N gauge Santa Fe Mallet on the layout of M. H. Consen.

Above: Talybont station on the narrow gauge OOn9 layout of David and Robin Edwards.

Left: Merebrook Station on the narrow gauge HO 9 layout operated by the Macclesfield Model Railway Society.

the motor, and this normally entailed delivering AC current. In many instances the locomotive contained a reversing switch which changed the polarity of the motor, thus enabling the train to be reversed.

Remember, whatever system is used, the current must complete a circuit for the motor to operate and therefore any break in the flow of electricity, normally known as a short circuit, will interfere with this process. It is useful to have a circuit tester which can be purchased from most electrical stores. It normally comprises something that looks like a pair of tweezers with a bulb on top. By placing this on the two tracks of a two-rail system, when the power is turned on the bulb should light up, thus proving the circuit. The principle of two-rail traction is that the right hand rail is insulated from the left hand rail both through the wheels of the locomotive and, of course, through the sleepers or ties. For this reason the wheel centres and sleepers are normally made from a non-conducting material such as plastic. Otherwise the current would merely flow through one rail via the axles or sleepers and back to the power pack thus by-passing the motor. The third rail system does not require

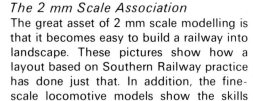

The 2 mm Scale Association

The great asset of 2 mm scale modelling is that it becomes easy to build a railway into landscape. These pictures show how a layout based on Southern Railway practice has done just that. In addition, the fine-scale locomotive models show the skills involved.

Top: Southern Railway T9 4-4-0 by John Greenwood powered by a Minitrix motor in the tender.

Centre, above: SR Class N 2-6-0 under construction by John Greenwood.

Above: SR 700 Class Black Motor 0-6-0 by John Greenwood.

Right: T9 approaching Bodmin on John Greenwood's 2 mm scale layout.

Left: Beattie well-tank on a short van train on John Greenwood's layout.

Below: 'O2' 2-4-4 T pulls into creamery halt on John Greenwood's layout.

Bottom: Bodmin station on John Greenwood's layout. It is hard to realise that such a spacious scene occupies a baseboard only one foot wide.

insulating material between the wheels or other tracks, the circuit being completed by the current flowing back through either outside track. As previously mentioned collection is a far greater problem with N gauge trains and to a lesser extent with HO trains than with an O gauge system. The weight of an O gauge engine would normally deal with any minor obstructions such as dust or particles of dirt. As a general rule if dirt and other material are major problems, as say in a garden railway, then a third rail system is more reliable, if less realistic.

Signals:

Choice of signalling will, of course, depend on the period being modelled. If the layout is intended to represent the prime years, then the semaphore type (swinging arm) will be the most suitable for that period. As with all signals, these can be manually operated (as most were in real life) and any vintage train collector will be familiar with the marvellous early tinplate signals, massively out of scale, many of them incorporating real oil lamps shining through the red or green glass of the semaphore. In the 1930s there were various attempts to attach signals to points and points to manual signal boxes by way of a system of rods and levers, but these systems gave way to fully automated signalling which was interlocked with point movements through a series of relays. Colour light signalling has, in many parts of the world, been commonplace for many years, but its application to model railways was only perfected in the 1930s and Marklin in particular pro-

A further three photographs of Cliff Young's HO gauge 3.5 mm scale 'Rio Grande in Miniature' (see also page 72).

Top: General view of Denver's Union station.

Centre: Eye-level views of Denver's Union station with Akane 4-8-2 No 1507 with the Mountaineer *on track 3.*

Above: No 3367 — a United 2-6-6-0 switching at Pine Cliff.

Left: Merebrook in Miniature. *A scene on the narrow gauge HO scale layout of Macclesfield Model Railway Society. This is a general view of the village of Merebrook.*

duced a vast range of colour light signals for their O gauge range. With the widespread acceptance of HO gauge, fully automated colour light signals became a normal part of the layout and today these have developed to a point where they can be operated on pre-set programmes, thereby allowing the railway to 'run itself'.

Usually these pre-programmed interlocking systems are operated by various trips set off by the train passing over a particular piece of track. Although it is almost impossible to see this 'trick', it only approximates the manner in which the systems work on a real railway. Signalling in model railways — apart from giving a line-side effect, thereby enhancing the authenticity of the line — is, on relatively advanced layouts, an intergral part of the system. As in real railways, the areas of track are designated as sections. Whereas the signalling of real railways is concerned with train movements and control, the sectioning in model railways is chiefly concerned with the ability to isolate a given section electrically. Through a point movement, a section of track can be isolated, that is, made dead, thereby automatically avoiding collisions by trains on adjoining sections. The principle of turning off engines through a central control panel is not one that is practical in real railways, which of course employ various track-operated brake devices, that operate when, for example, a driver totally ignores a signal instruction. In model railway terms, these equate more nearly with rather crude trip brake mechanisms on vintage clockwork railways.

Modernisation in Miniature

D. Bowes 4 mm scale model of British Railways London Midland Region uses the electric and diesel motive power of today. The track is by Peco using Peco point motors.

Right: A busy scene under the wires at a rural station made from Continental kits.

Top: The motive power depot is Hornby Dublo and Tri-ang.

Above: Diesel power parade.

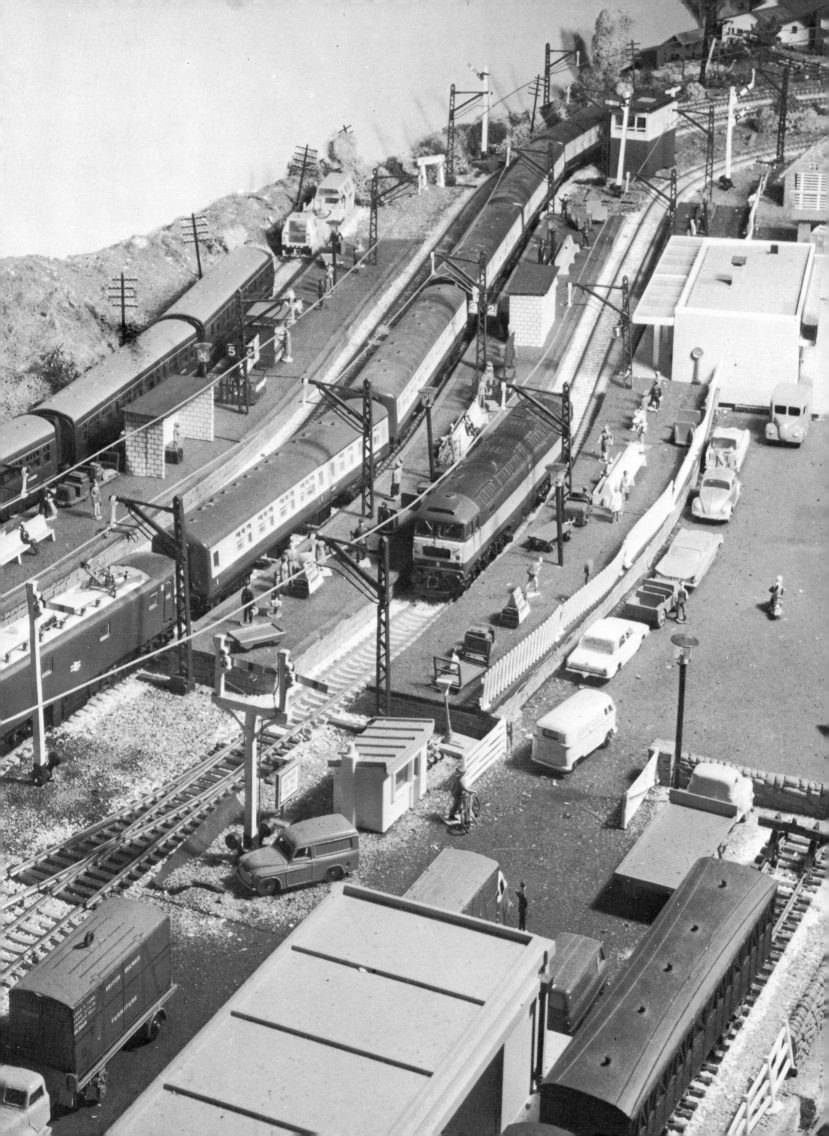

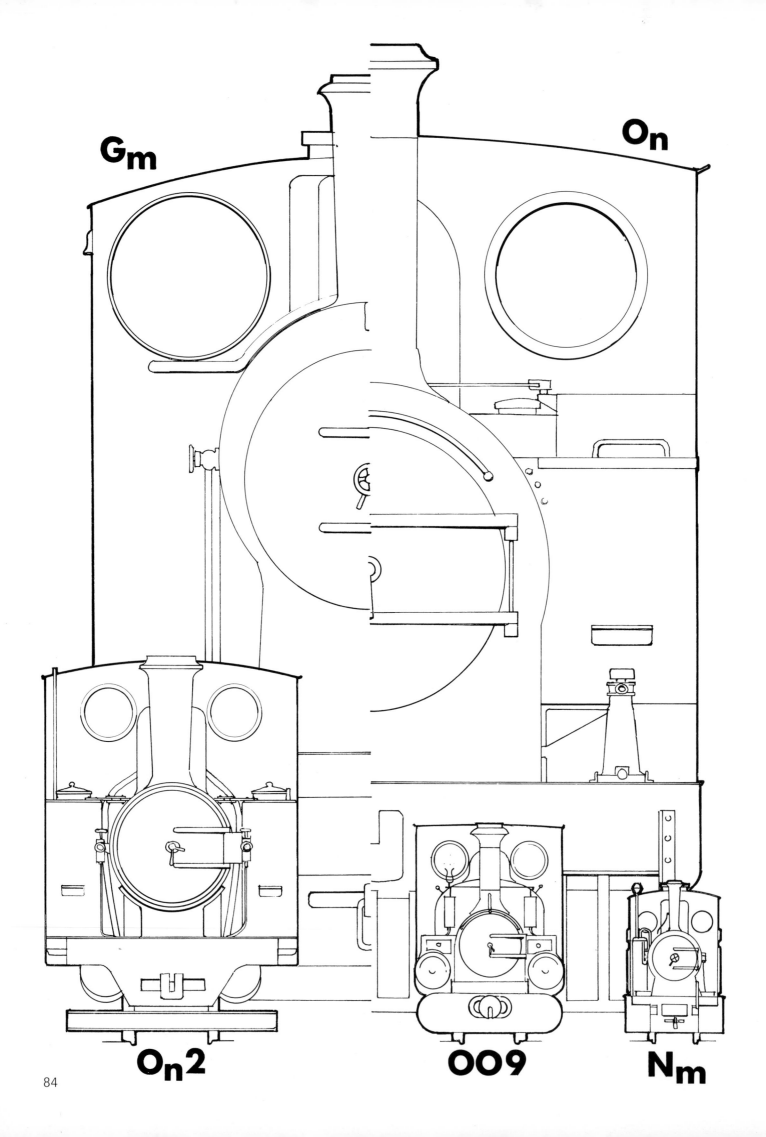

Gm

On

On2

OO9

Nm

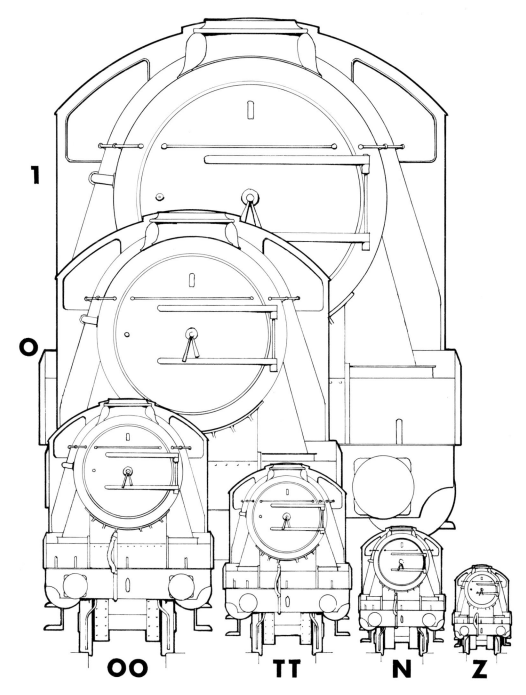

1

O

OO   **TT**   **N** **Z**

Above: The relative sizes (to scale) of a locomotive modelled in gauges 1, O, OO, TT, N and Z.

Left: Relative dimensions as applied to narrow gauge models.

G_m: RTM Werkspoor 0-6-0T 1/22.5 scale, Gauge 1 track.
On: Sierra Leone Rlys. Hunslet 2-6-2T, 14 mm/ft scale, O gauge track.
On2: WD Hunslet 4-6-0T, 1/48 scale, ½" gauge (or TT) track.
009: Penrhyn Rly. Hunslet 0-4-0T Linda, 4 mm scale, N gauge track.
N_m: RTM Orenstein 0-6-0T, 1/150 scale, Z gauge track.

Below: A Great Western Railway King stands head-on with American prototypes showing the relative sizes of British OO (standard), American OO (little used) and American HO (standard).

American OO

British OO   **American HO**

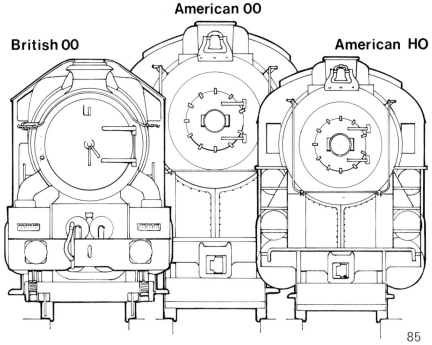

Name of Gauge	Gauge Width	Scale or Ratio	Remarks
Vintage			
O	32 mm	7 mm to 1 ft	The European gauge and scale which reached its height in popularity during the 1930s.
1	1¾ in	10 mm to 1 ft (UK) Scale ratio 1:32 (USA & Germany)	This gauge reached its peak before the First World War. Recently it has enjoyed a revival mainly in the specialist market. Particularly suitable for live steam operation outdoors. (1 ft is accepted on the fine-scale standard by the Gauge 1 MRA).
2	2 in	$\frac{7}{16}$ in to 1 ft Scale ratio 1:26	A short-lived gauge, now of more interest to collectors than operators.
3	2½ in	½ in to 1 ft	One of the first widely adopted gauges. Locomotives were principally steam fired and whereas commercially this gauge became extinct around 1912, it is still used by model engineers as one of the smallest practical gauges for coal-fired passenger-hauling locos.
4	3 in	35 mm to 1 ft	Very much a collectors' gauge and probably the rarest of all the large commercial gauges. Principally used by Bing and Schoenner.
American Vintage			
O	1¼ in	¼ in to 1 ft	This scale results in models being slightly smaller than their European counterparts, but for all practical purposes the gauge is virtually the same.
1	1¾ in	1:32	Made popular in the early part of the century, then abandoned by virtually every US manufacturer.
Standard	2⅛ in	⅜ in to 1 ft	The vintage gauge of America, it virtually disappeared after 1939.
S	⅞ in	1:64	Gilbert American Flyer was famous for marketing S gauge trains. While not strictly speaking vintage, S gauge products are now highly collectable.
Miniature and Sub Miniature			
OO	16.5 mm	4 mm to 1 ft 1:76.2	This gauge has been the most popular throughout the world. However the 4 mm scale is almost entirely confined to England. Even though OO gauge railways were originally designed for the UK market, the rest of the world has adopted HO, i.e. 3.5 mm to 1 ft, as the scale for trains running on 16.5 mm track.
HO	16.5 mm	3.5 mm to 1 ft 1:87.1	See notes above. This is still the most popular gauge and scale throughout the world.
TT3	12 mm	3 mm to 1 ft	A sub-miniature gauge first introduced by Tri-ang in the 1950s, now virtually obsolete. A very active 3 mm Society still exists with over 1000 members who regularly sponsor kits and parts. A secondary standard of the 3 mm Society is known as Scale 3 (S3)
TT	12 mm	2.5 mm to 1 ft	As with HO/OO the gauges are the same, but the preferred scales in Europe and the USA are different. As with TT3 this gauge is rarely seen today, although it is still very popular in Eastern Bloc countries where it is more common than N gauge.
OOO	9.5 mm	2 mm to 1 ft	The first of the truly sub-miniature gauges first introduced commercially as a relatively crude system (in fact 2 mm scale) by Lone Star in the 1950s. It was also adopted by an American group who still continue to model in this gauge, and they are served by a few highly specialised manufacturers. Historically OOO was first introduced as an amateurs' gauge in 1926 by H. R. Whaal. As with TT3 there is quite a large 2 mm scale association with an international membership which also sponsors kits and parts for members.
N	9 mm	1:148 mm (UK) 1:160 mm (USA & Europe)	The first sub-miniature gauge to seriously challenge OO/HO since the Second World War. Introduced in the 1960s, most leading manufacturers now list N gauge equivalents to most of their HO equipment.
Z	6.5 mm	1:220 mm	This is likely to define the final miniaturisation of commercially produced model trains. Introduced by Marklin in 1972 it is a system unique to that manufacturer.
Narrow Gauge			
Gm	45 mm	22.5 mm to 1 ft	A highly successful system introduced by LGB in 1968. It runs on track approximately equal to gauge 1.
On	32 mm	16 mm to 1 ft 14 mm to 1 ft 10 mm to 1 ft	A composite description for narrow gauge prototypes representing 2 ft, 2 ft 3 in and 3 ft types using scales as indicated. Thus the track is common to all these variants, but of course the size of the equipment differs.
On3	19 mm	1:48	The largest of the three standard narrow gauge systems used in the US.
On2	½ in	1:48	Another US standard narrow gauge.

Name of Gauge	Gauge Width	Scale or Ratio	Remarks
HOn3	10.5 mm	1.87:1	See above.
OUn3	12 mm	4 mm to 1 ft	A scale that enables modellers to model the 3 ft gauges still being used in the Isle of Man.

Fine Scale

Name of Gauge	Gauge Width	Scale or Ratio	Remarks
OF	32 mm	1:43.5	This represents the fine scale standards set by the French firm of Marescot in the 1920s. It is an attempt to achieve greater fidelity in flange thicknesses, track radii and point clearances. A British fine scale society known as Scaleseven (S7) exists.
EEM	18.83 mm	4 mm to 1 ft	A definitive gauge for fine scale OO modellers now known as Protofour (P4) and Scalefour (S4). Both these standards are basically exact 4 mm reproductions of full size dimensions. Each has its own society.
EM	18 mm	4 mm to 1 ft	This gauge was adopted by British modellers in an attempt to rectify the errors in the gauge/scale relationship of traditional OO equipment, i.e. 4 mm to 1 ft running on 3.5 mm track.

Above: The main line on the N gauge Continental (German) layout of F. Wilkinson. This aerial view shows a main line express and the local train ambling along beside the river in the valley.

Below: Proprietory Airfix 4 mm scale GWR 2-6-2T. The gauge is 18.23 mm and additional features include Mikes models wheels, Cambrian screw link couplings, 'Kings Cross' number plates.

Chapter 3
MOTIVE POWER

Toy trains were produced even before they were mechanised, the motive power being supplied by a simple human push or pull along the floor or around ready-formed circles of track.

The three principal forms of motive power for model railways have over the years comprised clockwork, steam and electricity. Apart from a few clockwork 'starter' railways, this form of motive power has all but disappeared as a commercially produced form of propulsion.

Clockwork

In Europe the first mass-produced commercial model railways were nearly all powered by clockwork, and historically the early toy train makers had close links with the Bavarian clock industry. It is, therefore, no coincidence that the pioneer train makers grew up in the Nuremburg district, an area already famous and 'geared up' for the manufacture of this form of mechanism.

A similar correlation occurred on the East Coast of America, although early toy makers were equally influenced by the presence of a colony of tinsmiths located in the New England area. In America the clockwork train is known as a 'wind up' or more generally as a mechanical toy. Gebrüder Bing, Marklin, Carette et Cie, the principal German pioneers, and later Bassett-Lowke and Hornby in England all produced clockwork-powered locomotives in their ranges and gauge O clockwork versions of Hornby trains were available until the early 1950s.

The great disadvantage of clockwork was the lack of control that could be exercised by the operator. Various relatively sophisticated control mechanisms were devised over the years; among them was the British Walker Fenn mechanism which enabled a locomotive to be set to run at very low speeds, thereby creating more realism. Bassett-Lowke also adopted a variable speed control mechanism and other manufacturers included trip devices built into the rails in order to stop and start clockwork engines. None of these variations, however, offered the magic ingredient – remote control. While there is little doubt that in the early days of model railways clockwork railways were the safest for youthful operators and furthermore relatively easy to set up after father had ordered the floor to be cleared, they succumbed in an advancing world to the joys and hazards of electricity. If you choose to buy clockwork remember, do not overwind, oil regularly and do not run the locomotive with its wheels off the track, i.e. without the friction of the rails acting as a 'damper' to the unwinding of the spring.

Steam

As a means of propelling model trains, steam arrived on the scene at about the same time as clockwork. Initially (before the prolific 'dribblers') model steam locomotives tended to be rather grand beasts, usually built in brass and indeed, in the late 19th century, the British and French instrument makers were the first to offer significant ranges of track and trackless steam locomotives. They were invariably spirit fired, the flame being delivered externally through a spirit-soaked wick to the outside of the boiler. Safety was not of great moment, although some models were internally fired, the heat being delivered through flues built into the boiler. A development of this method was the highly efficient smithies boiler (see illustration). Locomotives powered by steam were offered commercially in gauges O to 4 (see table) and although many significant coal-fired models were built in these gauges, they were normally the work of advanced amateur builders and were only offered by commercial companies as very expensive one-off or small-batch productions. Large scale production of steam locomotives was almost totally confined to Europe and Bing, Marklin, Carette and Ernst Plank were the principal suppliers.

In the 1920s Bassett-Lowke, who until that time had taken their products from the German factories, initiated a fine range of gauge O steam locomotives and these were available until the late 1960s. Whereas most model steam locomotives were sold principally for use in the home, they could also be used outdoors for garden railways. However, operating at relatively low pressures, they were greatly influenced by climatic conditions and, indeed, a strong gust of wind would tend to extinguish the flame and a low ambient temperature would cause much thermal loss. Nonetheless, the more successful variants could, in ideal conditions, run for twenty minutes or more with just one filling of spirit and water. The Bassett-Lowke range of spirit-fired locomotives, in particular, was designed in such a way that the spirit would be used up before the boiler ran dry, thus avoiding one of the inherent dangers of a pot-boilered model steam locomotive, namely that the boiler could turn into a projectile if the water ran out while the boiler was still being vigorously heated. In recent years manufacturers have been turning their attention once again to the production of model steam locomotives. Concurrent with this writing (as previously mentioned), a steamable HO model of a 'Rocket' is being marketed and it is likely that this will be followed by other examples of the genre as the quest for realism and/or novelty continues.

Right: Tri-ang Railways were the first all-plastic, two-rail systems for the mass UK market. Introduced in the 1950s, their sales rapidly overhauled Hornby Dublo, the undisputed leaders in that field. The reasons were twofold. Firstly their two-rail system was more realistic and secondly, the adoption of plastic injection moulding techniques gave them a distinct price advantage on Hornby's metal-based products.

Below: An example of the use of proprietary equipment to assist in the making of an unusual prototype model. D. Mallinson's HO gauge 3.5 mm scale, scratch-built model of a French de Glehn compound 4-6-0 using Hornby Dublo driving wheels. An engine of this class can be seen on the preserved Nene Valley Railway.

LOCOMOTIVES AND PASSENGER ROLLING STOCK

Tri-ang Railways "TT" Gauge rolling stock is superbly detailed and finished in authentic colours. Automatic couplings are fitted to all rolling stock permitting automatic coupling and uncoupling to be undertaken by means of Uncoupling Tracks. Heavy metal bogies and chassis ensure smooth running at all speeds.

T.90 0-6-0 Class 3F Tank Loco. **31/-**

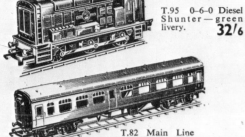

T.95 0-6-0 Diesel Shunter — green livery. **32/6**

T.130 S.R. Suburban Composite Coach. **7/3**
T.80 (not. illus.) Suburban Composite Coach—maroon. **7/3**

T.184 W.R. Restaurant Car. **10/2**
T.84 (not illus.) Restaurant Car—maroon. **9/7**
T.134 (not illus.) S.R. Restaurant Car. **9/7**

T.82 Main Line Composite Coach—maroon. **7/3**
T.132 (not illus.) S.R. Main Line Composite Coach. **7/3**
T.182 (not illus.) W.R. Main Line Composite Coach. **7/7**

T.91 4-6-0 "Windsor Castle" Loco—green livery. **48/-**
T.92 Tender for T.91. **6/3**

T.133 S.R. Main Line Brake 2nd Coach. **7/3**
T.83 (not illus.) Main Line Brake 2nd Coach—maroon. **7/3**
T.183 (not illus.) W.R. Main Line Brake 2nd Coach. **7/7**

T.93 4-6-2 "Merchant Navy" Class Loco—green livery. **50/9**
T.94 Tender for T.93. **6/7**

T.81 Suburban Brake 2nd Coach—maroon. **7/3**
T.131 (not illus.) S.R. Suburban Brake 2nd Coach. **7/3**

T.96 A-1-A—A-1-A Diesel Electric Loco—green livery. **52/6**

DO YOU KNOW? *British Transport Commission's Ships Number 116*

American manufacturers have over the years flirted with the model steam engine and Beggs, Garlick and Weedon have achieved some success in this field. One American manufacturer, the Steam and Electric Company of Blomfield, New Jersey, adapted a Weedon locomotive and a Lionel tender to run on an immersion heater principle, namely it took up the power to heat the boiler element from the track. Properly developed this could, of course, have overcome one of the principal problems of small scale steam locomotives, namely inefficient and relatively dangerous firing procedures. But the inherent problems of water with electricity made this American idea an unlikely challenge. Furthermore, this system required relatively high currents to heat the element efficiently.

It is interesting to note that since the disappearance of batch-produced model steam locomotives in the 1960s, several specialist firms have successfully marketed very fine batches of live-steam locomotives, mainly for gauge 1 Among these Wilag of Switzerland (who marketed a superb butane gas fired Pacific) and Astor of Japan were to produce outstanding steam-powered models. If you choose steam, test the safety valve regularly and never screw it down completely. Keep the lubricator topped up and fill the boiler with WATER. Do *not* leave the model unattended with small children.

Electricity – Mains and Battery

The first known model train (or electric train of any kind) was made in 1835 by Thomas Davenport, the inventor of the electric motor. The first electric streetcar ran in Montgomery, Alabama in 1886 and in 1895 the Baltimore and Ohio Railway put the first electric locomotives into regular service. Incidentally, the B & O were to provide prototypes for London's first electric railway – the Central London Railway – and thus provide the outline for the first mass-produced toy electric outline trains, put out by both Bing and Marklin at the turn of the century (although initially these were clockwork powered). The first recorded patent on a toy electric railway was dated 1884. This patent was taken out by the Novelty Electric Company of Philadelphia, but it does not appear to have been put into production.

The first electric toy locomotive produced in quantity is generally believed to have been manufactured by Ernst Plank around 1890, and this was a most whimsical affair which sported a striped canopy. Garlick, an early American toy train maker, also produced an extraordinary steeple-cab-type locomotive at this time, but it was not until the early part of the 20th century that electric propulsions for model trains became acceptable.

America was to embrace electricity, and thus the electric train, far earlier and more comprehensively than Europe and, indeed, the electric train, whether in proper outline or as a series for powering steam outline locomotives always far outstripped sales of either clockwork or steam-propelled model trains, which in Europe enjoyed great vogue. Electric model railways have now developed in such a way that they virtually dominate the mass market and for all practical purposes the system in one form or another is universal.

Although the first electric trains were powered by batteries, the almost universal availability of mains electricity has reduced this system to a very minor role.

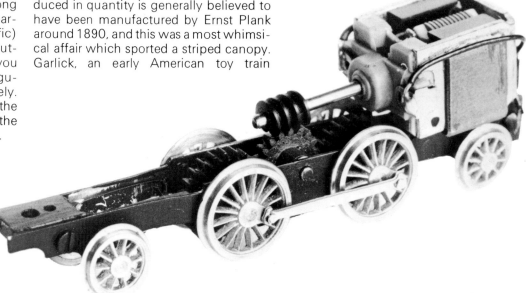

Above: A 2 mm scale 9.42 mm gauge chassis for an LNER F4 2-4-2T built by Mike Bigant of the 2 mm Scale Association. The motor is the standard Fleischmann N gauge and gears are available through the association.

Right: This electromotive diesel switcher model was produced by General Models in 1947–48. (This same model is still available from All-Nation Hobby in Chicago — about 30 years of kit longevity.)

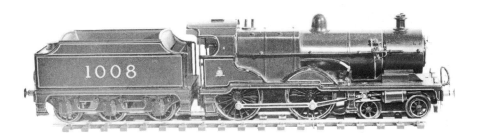

Nonetheless, there are still regions of the world without a suitable supply of mains electricity, but where people still wish to play trains. Its other main area of acceptance is in the field of 'starter' train sets, as not only are battery-powered systems cheaper to run, but also they are obviously safer.

Most major manufacturers afford a dual capability for their controllers to be linked up to batteries or mains, but a controller made specifically for battery operation cannot, normally, be mains operated. Whereas battery power is fine for a simple circle of track, it becomes less viable when many accessories are to be worked by remote control, as any significant increase on the power demanded from the normal 12 volt battery soon shortens its life. Today, of course, recharging batteries is commonplace, but generally it would be pointless to charge a battery all night off the mains in order to run a small model railway off it the next day.

Left from top to bottom:

Class 2 4-4-0 No 509. *This is an improved CCW kit with a Reader motor.*

MR 0-10-0 banking engine. *This reproduction of the famous Lickey Barker was scratch built. To enable the locomotive to negotiate 3' 0" radius curves the first and fifth axles have a 2 mm movement either side of the frames.*

Midland Railway 0-6-0 well tank. *The chassis and boiler show the method of construction used by Rex Rose. The wheels and axle are fully sprung with axle box movement in the horns. Very little solder was used, most of the members being screwed. The mechanism is a cut down version of a Rocket Precision.*

Somerset & Dorset Joint Railway 2-8-0. *This model was constructed side by side with the MR 0-10-0 and has a similar 2 mm play in the 4th driving axle to allow it to negotiate 3' 0" radius curves. The motor is a rewound Bonds mounted on ball races.*

Compound 4-4-0 No 1008. *A completely rebuilt Bassett-Lowke model fitted with a Mills motor. The livery is that of the Midland Railway from 1907–1922.*

Fine Scale Models in 7 mm Scale

The late Hamilton Bantock was an example of how determination can make an amateur into a skilled craftsman. A policeman by profession, Bantock was taught the fine arts of workshop practice by that exquisite modeller, Rex Rose, late in life. These models, all representing Midland Railway locomotives are examples of his art. A policeman's eye is one used to detail.

Chapter 4
FIRST STEPS

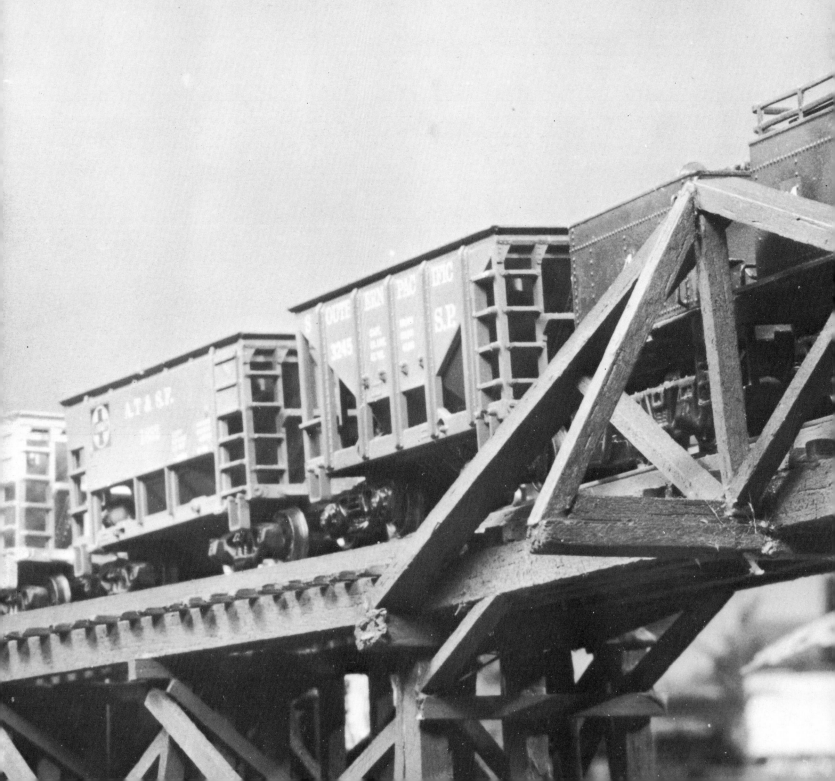

Having described the historical background to the electric train, let us now consider the problem of choice. Taking the archetype situation first — father who is longing to return to model trains eagerly awaits his son's appropriate birthday (sometimes his first!). A visit to the neighbourhood hobby or toy shop inevitably results in the purchase of a train set. It seldom ends there. In most cases the train set is attractively packaged, and its primary intention is to involve the purchaser with that particular manufacturer's offerings. It is designed as a temporary layout in so far as it is taken to pieces after play and, hopefully, replaced neatly in its box. An intermediate stage between the temporary model railway and the permanent layout can be achieved by purchasing a pre-formed baseboard with all the trackways moulded into a simulated landscape, including tunnels, ramps, etc. The advantage of this is that it avoids the necessity of constructing the basic scenery, levels, ramps and tunnels. The principal disadvantage is the inflexibility of such a pre-formed baseboard, although certain manufacturers offer extension boards which can be butted up to one another thereby enabling a degree of expansion. Nevertheless, the trackways are pre-determined and usually designed to take a particular manufacturer's equipment, i.e. Noch layout dioramas are best suited to Fleischmann equipment.

From the temporary and pre-formed baseboard, a quantum leap in model railways is to the one-off system fashioned to the owner's own fantasy — or taking it one stage further, modelling a railway on a known section of actual railway. Often the problem of scale makes the choice a compromise between fantasy and reality, and it must be borne in mind that here we are dealing primarily with indoor model railway systems, where space is usually at some sort of premium.

Gauge and Space

The next obvious question is 'which gauge?' A small collection of O gauge? A fairly complicated OO/HO system in the same space, or an even larger and possibly extremely complex N gauge railway, once again in a roughly equivalent space?

Assuming an average space of 10 feet by 8 feet the following plans could be adopted. Once the decision has been made to construct a permanent railway, the most important consideration is the construction of the baseboard and for this purpose it must be assumed that a particular room, or more normally a loft, has been commandeered for the purpose, as it is desirable to fix the feet of the baseboards to the floor to avoid movement and limit vibration.

It is possible, of course, to construct a

Layout on a Bookcase
David Howsam's intriguing idea for a model railway in the living room. The bookcase stands on the floor and the railway model is contained in the top fold-away section.

Left: The bookcase.

Below: The bookcase transformed into the 4 mm scale layout ready for operating.

Right: A closeup of the model.

baseboard layout on a portable base, and indeed many marvellous and complex layouts may be seen at clubs and exhibitions in the sub-miniature gauges, i.e. N gauge. It is even possible to build an interesting railway that folds into a piece of furniture or performs beneath the glass of a small table. Both the large portable and the very individual miniature systems are either the result of a group effort or have a degree of gimmickry about them. For most people — and particularly those who wish to have a trouble-free, instantly available model railway — the permanent baseboard system offers many advantages.

The traditional baseboard is a solid wooden board which is smooth, flat and well braced to avoid annoying tremors. Its construction is a relatively simple matter yet is worthy of some thought and pre-planning if it is to form the ideal base for one's model and be of optimum size. There is nothing worse than having a baseboard which is either too big for the particular room in which the model is sited or so wide that parts of the finished model cannot be easily reached. Just as frustrating is the base which turns out to be too small to take all one had planned for it. Consider, therefore, the size of the room and what you are intending to have in it in terms of permanent way, buildings

and other scenic effects. At the same time, bear in mind the scale of the model and the 'real' area which it is intended to represent. A length of track can often be made to look longer than it really is by placing it on a narrow baseboard.

Having considered these points it is best then to draw a scale plan of the room and the baseboard and proposed layout to work out the feasibility of your ideas. While you will doubtless be anxious not to have to purchase more board than necessary, on grounds of cost if nothing else, it is an unwise modeller who skimps; almost certainly he will find that sections which have been cut too narrow and not properly braced have warped and will need to be replaced in a few months to give good running conditions.

There are many advantages to the traditional semi-permanent, solid baseboard — i.e., one that will remain *in situ* most of the time but can be moved if necessary: its very solidity provides security, a safe and square surface which assists good running and one which, if necessary can be stood upon with impunity. In addition, the basic solid top can always be cleared of one layout and replaced with another.

What type of materials should be used for this sort of baseboard? Essentially one is looking for something which is not too

hard, since it will have to be drilled and track pins will need to be positioned, and not too soft for obvious reasons. Half-inch thick Sundeala and Karlitpanel marine grade (BSS 1088) are ideal, easy to work and will accept panel pins. For bracing, 2-inch by 1-inch timber is indisputably the best for preventing twisting and warping. When buying material both for the baseboard and the bracing it is more economical to purchase to the nearest foot or, since many timber merchants have now turned to metric measurement, nearest meter and, for the former, to use pre-cut sheets since nowadays one has to pay extra for cutting to size, usually at so much per cut. To avoid waste — and frustration later! — always check your measurements, particularly before starting to cut; it is surprising how much waste can be incurred by a hasty cut made without checking.

Having settled on the shape and size of the base begin its construction by making a frame for the top. The timber should be used with the 2 inch as its upright measurement and the 1 inch as its width since this provides the maximum bearing strength. The sides of the frame should be made first, each with a rebate of $\frac{1}{2}$ inch at either end to take the end-pieces. Next prepare the cross-braces or bearers to provide additional support for the board and give further protection against warping and twisting. Again, rebate the side pieces, this time to a 1-inch depth and also cut rebates to the same depth on the ends of the bearers. (See illustration A). Remember that the longer and wider the base, the more bearers will be required and that the greater the width, the closer together the bearers should be placed.

Though nails can be used on the joints they are not entirely satisfactory since they present a danger of splitting the ends of the wood and also of working loose. Screws provide a more permanent joint and it is best to use two for each corner joint and one for each side-to-bearer joint, drilling holes in the receiving piece of wood (the piece which the screw enters first) and countersinking them so that the screwheads do not protrude. For greater strength, glue the joints before inserting the screws, using a good wood glue. The frame is now ready to receive the top, the shape of which should be clearly drawn out before cutting. Here, too, though nails can be used to fasten the board to the frame, screws provide a more durable fixture and again holes should be driiled and countersunk.

With the top complete it must now be provided with its support. The ideal height of the baseboard from floor level is around 3 feet 6 inches, though this will vary with the individual. Support can be provided either by means of trestles (homemade or shop-bought) or of legs

HO scale: Sierra Railroad 2-8-0 and train in scenic surroundings.

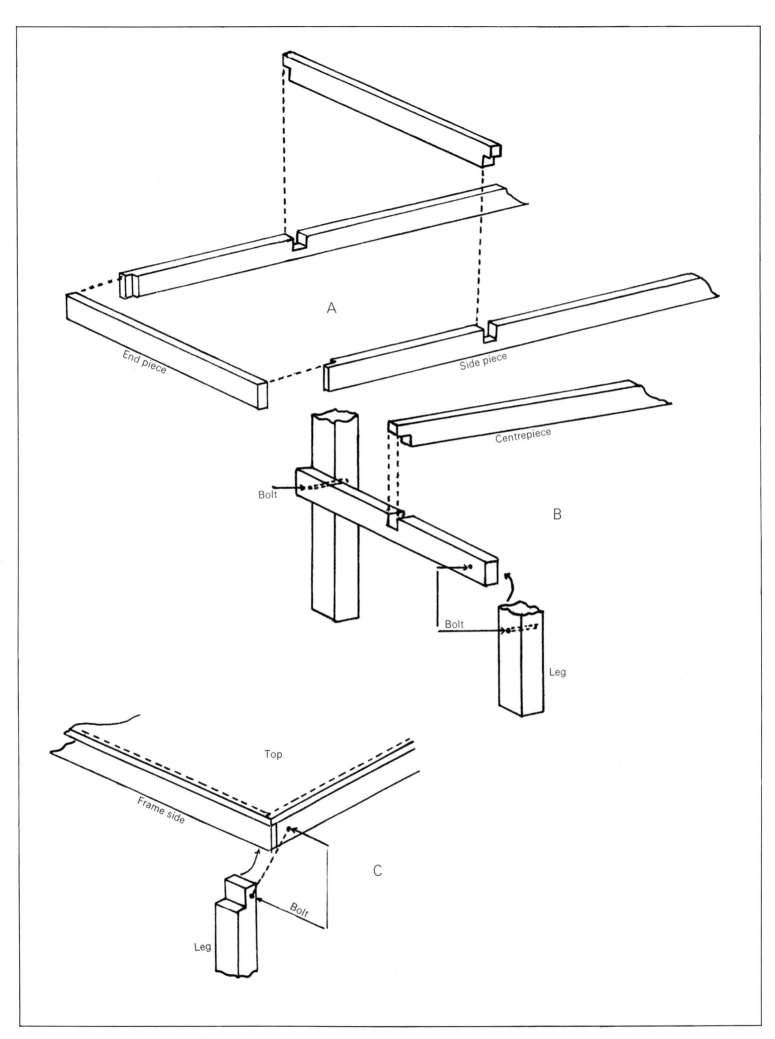

A

End piece

Side piece

Centrepiece

Bolt

Bolt

Leg

B

Top

Frame side

Bolt

Leg

C

at each corner, held vertical and given extra rigidity by means of a stretcher. Ideally, the legs should be made from 2 inch by 2 inch timber, while the stretcher can be of the same 2 inch by 1 inch timber used for the baseboard frame.

The legs should *not* be attached to the baseboard itself since the weight of the board and contents will then be transmitted directly through the legs, almost certainly causing lifting at the corners. The intention is that the weight of the whole top should be spread through its frame and down the legs. Hence the 2 inch by 2 inch timber is cut to fit inside the frame — but half an inch or so below the baseboard — and rebated to form a step upon which the bottom of the side of the frame will fit. (See illustration B).

The stretcher is simple to construct, making its two ends exactly the same length as the width of the baseboard and the centrepiece as long as the board. Again, the timber is used with the 2 inch as the upright measurement and the ends of the centrepiece and centres of the two end-pieces are rebated 1 inch each, drilled, countersunk, glued and screwed. It is essential to make the joints a good, strong fit since the stretcher will take a good deal of strain. (See illustration C). Bolt the completed stretcher to the legs at about 10 to 12 inches from the floor and then, after clamping the legs to the frame, drill through the thickness of the leg and the frame and insert a bolt through each of these holes. Use $\frac{3}{8}$-inch coach bolts in each position with a washer, nut and locking nut and make sure that if a square-necked bolt is used it bites home into the wood. Now bolt the legs to the frame in the positions already prepared.

There is no need to fasten the whole thing to the wall and many modellers will want to fix a backscene to the baseboard before placing it in position. This can be made from $\frac{1}{4}$-inch plywood which can be nailed — since it is not going to take any strain — to the back side-piece of the frame and can stand some 9 to 12 inches high. For still greater stability the legs can be fitted with 3-inch angle irons which are screwed to the floor once the completed unit has been set in its chosen position.

Wiring is very much a matter for the individual but points which are worth bearing in mind are that mains leads should never be left trailing or placed in positions where they can be snagged or become worn, and layout wiring should be hidden as much as possible by running it under the baseboard and through holes drilled in the frame members. They can be held in position with insulated electrical staples or, if they are grouped, by larger garden staples.

One final point to bear in mind is that many floors are not level. It is, therefore, wise to check for irregularities and pack

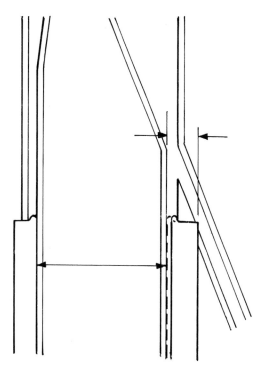

Top: Wheel profiles reduced to the same scale.

Above: The critical dimensions of wheels and track.

beneath the legs of the unit where necessary, checking with a spirit level in several places on the top to ensure that the whole thing is level.

Making one's own baseboard does not, of course, preclude the average modeller from using proprietary scenic and lineside effects. It is, however, likely that the modeller will wish to model the more significant features of his landscape. Many European model railway landscapes include at least one alp, although in scale terms few, if any model railways could ever contain such an edifice. A modest mountain, say 10,000 feet on an HO layout would require a ceiling height of some 350 metres! The construction of scenery will depend on the degree of realism required. Chicken wire shaped in the form of hills and covered with cellulose base cloth, medical lint or hessian (the coarseness of the material would have to match the scale of the railway) soaked in plaster of paris, is a time-honoured method of recreating the essential texture of a landscape. The contours are then coloured by hand or sprinkled with pre-coloured sand and glue or one of the many proprietary plastic-based flocks. Trees may be constructed from wire and pre-coloured sponge or, once again the modeller may prefer to purchase some of the many realistic trees, usually formed in plastic, available at most railway hobby stores. Conifers are particularly effective in this medium. Further hints on scenic effects are given later.

The Permanent Way

The permanent way can be a misnomer when applied to model railways as most youthful modellers will know the agony of having to break up a model railway line that has entwined itself under and around most of the furniture in the main living room. Therefore, in any construction of model railway track, the following should be borne in mind. Is the railway required to be dismantled at regular intervals or does it conform to the ideal, and form part of a permanent layout.

Track, like any other part of model railways, can be built virtually from scratch. To this end manufacturers have, for many years, provided wooden sleepers, accurately cast chairs, and the correct rail sections for the various scales. In the case of the absolute purist nothing other than the hand-assembled trackway, contoured to fit his exact requirements will do. For the intermediate modeller, the pre-formed flexible plastic sleeper and track provide an ideal solution between hand-made track and the rigid pre-formed track, available with most train sets. Track, of course, has always been the prime merchandise which had to be acquired if the system was to be expanded and as such manu-

*More HO scale: Climax locomotive with
ore cars on trestle bridge.*

Left: Electrification by outside third rail. Charlie Shoults' 7 mm scale model based on LNER practice. This form of third rail, made operative by using spring bar type collectors on the locomotive, was very popular prior to the introduction of stud contact and two rail systems.

Bottom far left: Electrification by stud contact. Bob Ledger's O gauge Manchester Central layout uses studs inserted between the rails at regular intervals connected, as shown in the photograph, with thin wire. The locomotive is fitted with long skate type collectors to bridge the gaps. For those not wishing to use the more ugly third rail and the more complicated two rail system this form of electrification is extremely practical.

Bottom centre: General view of Jamestown station on Manchester Model Railway Society's O gauge layout.

Above: Electrification by the two rail system. Some excellent track work on the Manchester Model Railway Society's 7 mm scale exhibition layout. Current is supplied to the locomotive's wheels rolling on the track; one rail is connected to the DC positive lead, the other to the negative. The locomotive's wheels (insulated from each other) act as pick-ups.

Left: Hand-built EM gauge trackwork at station throat, Marthwaite was originally built in 1963–65.

An HO scale layout (with Canadian connections) belonging to John B. Porter. Here a Sante Fe 2-8-0 pulls a train of hoppers while a Colorado and Southern locomotive crosses a bridge containing dual gauge tracks.

facturers over the years have paid great attention to the provision of ready-to-run track. In any major manufacturer's list the varieties of trackwork will usually compete with a variety of locomotives and rolling stock. Realising the essential nature of this product, some manufacturers have, in fact, become world-famous for their track alone and, indeed, Peco (Pritchard Patent Product Company) sell more track than any other model railway product. That firm was responsible for introducing the first plastic-sleepered, flexible track, and later the first universal track that would be suitable for virtually any type of wheel currently in mass production. Flexible track, which is now almost universal for anything but the pure train set market, must by its very nature be permanently fixed to a baseboard. This does not preclude the track being taken up and re-used in a different part of the railway or, indeed, on a completely new layout, but in order to hold its desired radius, it needs to be affixed to a rigid surface. This can be achieved in two ways, either by tacking the track directly on to the baseboard (not to be recommended) or by gluing the track to either a cork or sponge simulated ballast which is then fixed to the baseboard with adhesives. With a contemporary adhesive little else is required to achieve a permanent fixture, but nevertheless, it is recommended that small tacks be applied through the sleepers at intervals in order to give absolute rigidity.

Above: A magnificent example of 2 mm scale trackwork: realism in miniature.

Below: Working replicas of British Rail's colour light signals on D. Bowe's 4 mm scale layout based on modern British Rail practice.

Of course, no railway system can run without point-work or switches (see illustration). These are required to move a train on to a different track, and it goes without saying that without them one is faced with the prospect of going either round and round or up and down. Every point is two short lengths of movable track. Points are connected together and moved in tandem. The position of the points determines whether the train is to move straight on or turn to either the right or the left. For this reason they are designated as right hand and left hand. At its simplest, the point is moved manually by a lever, normally incorporated in the base of the trackwork. In a complicated railway system this obviously has disadvantages, but against that it has the merit of simplicity and is certainly more suited to the non-permanent railway. The remote control point is thrown electrically. In the case of most proprietary track points, the point motor is moulded within the track and merely requires to be coupled up to the accessory terminals of the power pack. In the case of more sophisticated model railways, the point motor is a separate component and in order to achieve maximum realism it is fixed to the underside of the baseboard with a hole drilled for the arm which is then the only visible part of the mechanism. Each point motor is then wired to a control panel, which in many instances will contain a diagram of the point layout, much in the same way as those appearing in real life signal boxes.

Right: A Club at Work — *Manchester Model Railway Society's 7 mm scale O gauge layout is designed to be worked as correctly as possible employing as many operators as it can — an ideal club working model railway. Here is Cornbrook locomotive yard, goods yard and main control panel with power pack and duplicate bank of relays.*

Below right: Sid Stubb's 4 mm fine-scale layout — Northchurch. Full view of underside of a baseboard section. The two cylindrical objects on the left are uncoupler electro-magnets. Point relays and plugs are clearly visible.

Below: Sid Stubb's of the Manchester Model Railway Society in his workshop. Note the importance of tidiness.

In a comprehensive layout, wiring of point motors in this way can result in highly complex wiring systems, and it is always necessary to colour code the wires, as without this guide it is almost impossible to locate faults such as short circuits. Apart from the relatively simple left and right hand points, model railway track follows its real life counterpart in almost every respect and crossovers, double crossovers, diagonal points, double slips and right angled crossovers have at most times been marketed by the model railway trade. In the early days even Bing marketed an improbable three-way triangular

point (see illustration) which must have come to the designer after a particularly heavy night in the Bavarian beer halls. It should not be confused with a proper three-way tandem or unilateral point.

Scenic and Scale Effects

Although scenery has been discussed very briefly, it is obvious that once a permanent baseboard-type layout has been established, then the scenery will form almost as important a feature of the railway as the actual trains themselves. In fact it is arguable that today N gauge railways al-

most present themselves as architectural dioramas. The fundamental mistake made by so many model railway enthusiasts is that they acquire masses of locomotives and rolling stock and find that within a short time their model railway resembles a monumental traffic jam giving neither pleasure nor realism. Ironically, this has been the course that has led many potential enthusiasts to become so intrigued with the hardware that they take on the guise of collector and the room designated for running railways becomes a veritable museum. While it is true in life that the best-laid plans can always go

Inset: A fine example of a prototype station building in 4 mm scale. Stan Robert's Bakewell based on Midland Railway practice on the route from Derby to Manchester.

An LMS Hughes 2-6-0 crosses a girder bridge on the 4 mm scale layout of the Newport Model Railway Society.

The Art of Compromise

There are many reasons for building and operating a model railway. Some prefer to concentrate on true scale replicas of branch lines; others, on a railway in the landscape; and some find their pleasure in running a collection of superb scale models. Another excellent reason is the special fascination of getting as close as possible to carrying out the day to day operations of a railway system. This is the thinking behind Keith Ladbury's 4 mm scale layout dealing with the Great Western Railway. With its London terminus at Paddington, trains radiate over the GWR system northwest to Birkenhead via Birmingham and west to Wales. This is done by means of a split-level system with the portions of the line between the stations representing towns, running in tunnels — the art of compromise. By building his railway in this fashion Keith Ladbury has been able to achieve his ambition and operates the layout as if he was able actually to run a railway.

1. A section of the layout showing the various levels.
2. Section above — Leicester station with LNER (GC) 4-4-2 tank and below 4708 2-8-0 *en route* to Birmingham.
3. Shrewsbury shed with Great Western, London and North Western and Cambrian locomotives.
4. Shrewsbury station.
5. A Dean Goods 0-6-0 approaches Welshpool.
6. Machynlleth station.
7. A Dean Goods 0-6-0 on Barmouth bridge *en route* to Machynlleth.
8. Swansea station.

wrong, it is very difficult to combine the collecting instinct with the realistic scenic model railway. What normally happens is that the collector gravitates to running vintage or tinplate trains, where realism is not a high priority while the serious scale modeller becomes totally involved with fidelity which, at its most refined can comprise a scale section of, say, one mile of real track or station buildings, with no more than half-a-dozen pieces of rolling stock. For this clan of enthusiast this can represent the highest achievement of the art. Here, therefore, we will deal briefly with the latter type of modeller as, of course, there are very few rules to apply when clipping together vintage tinplate track and placing marvellous, if monstrously out-of-scale buildings and accessories thereon.

The best way to commence the modelling of a scale railway is to research the period on which the railway is to be modelled. Obvious sources are contemporary photographs and books dealing with the particular railway stating which types of equipment were used and when. Ordinance survey maps, to a scale of 1:2500 are most useful to modellers. Contemporary railways and buildings are always marked on these maps and exact dimensions can be extrapolated. For a variety of reasons it is often impossible to achieve an exact scale model of a real life object. In the case of model railways continual debates are found in the correspondence columns of the various journals, and these often are reduced to highly academic mathematical arguments. Most of these arguments could be knocked on the head through the simple realisation that not even the real life objects were built to an absolutely constant scale. The very essence of modelling is the creation of effect and feeling and, therefore, when reducing a stretch of track which is 18 feet in length by up to a third, i.e. 6 feet, an equal illusion of distance may, in most instances be achieved. One of the greatest items of contention is the radii of curves. In the case of gauge O, fine-scale modelling was first introduced in the 1920s on minimum radius curves of 2,250 mm. Even in fine scale terms the thickness of a wheel is 3.75 mm compared to the actual prototype which, reduced by 1:43.5 (i.e. 7 mm to 1 foot), would give an actual measurement of 3 mm. These arguments are merely inserted to show that even at the purest level of modelling, absolute mathematical reduction in scale is not necessarily completely acceptable. After all, unless a railway can run efficiently – have wheels that are thick enough or provide sufficient adhesion, particularly through point work to collect the current – then all the arguments of scale are rendered meaningless. For average and even advanced modellers, therefore, optics are

even more important than mathematics. It is a general rule that the larger the wheelbase of the locomotive the more true to scale the radii of curves will need to be to operate railways efficiently. Even the coarsest tinplate railways recognised this, and Hornby were required to introduce a special 3-foot radius track to accommodate their famous Princess Elizabeth Pacific locomotive. As little as 9-inch radius curves suited some of their less glamorous offerings.

Buildings are obviously one of the most important features of a model railway and the modeller is thoroughly spoiled today with the vast range of both plastic and card-based kits that are available. However, the more specialist the area of modelling, the less likely it is that the manufacturers will produce buildings for a modeller in the area of his particular interest. Therefore, some, if not all of the buildings on a model railway will require to be scratch built. Colour is obviously the main consideration as bricks and rendering materials in various parts of the country differ enormously. Again the modeller may be helped here by the many printed sheets of building surfaces that are available in various scales from the hobby shops. Plans of a particular building are obviously difficult to come by, and here some licence may be necessary when scaling down outlines from photographs. Human figures obviously add life to a model railway and here too an enormous range of plastic figures, available from stores, are more than adequate for most modellers' purposes. Other ephemera such as advertising signs are now being marketed in sheet form and reproductions of the marvellous examples put out by Bassett-Lowke before the First World War, which were lithographed on to tinplate, are now being reproduced in paper form.

Water: Rivers, streams, ponds and lakes are all eye-catching elements of a model landscape, and a bridge across a stream or river is often more attractive than a similar construction across a road. Water, by its very nature is translucent and yet has a mirror-like quality when it reflects light. For very still water, glass is an ideal medium and for broader expanses of water, rippled glass, suitably coloured on the underside, will give a realistic effect. Failing these materials, the glossiest of paints applied very liberally to the baseboard can also be a very effective way to reproduce the illusion of water. Paint used in this way is further enhanced with a coat or two of shiny varnish.

Grass: As mentioned earlier, grass can be simulated by small granules of sawdust that have been dyed green or, alternatively natural sawdust can be dyed any

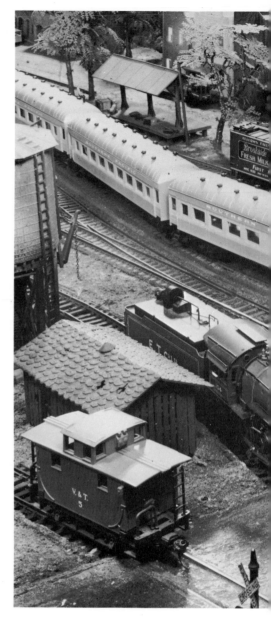

colour by using domestic clothes dye. If you are fortunate in finding sawdust from one of the dark woods such as mahogany or chestnut, then you have nature's own contribution to earth tones without the need for any further colouring. It is best to pre-glue the area to be grassed or earthed, with a white glue, using a broad brush. Then by putting the sawdust in a fine-screen strainer, it can be shaken gently over the required areas in an even layer on to the wet glue. When the glue has dried the excess sawdust can either be brushed or airblown off the surface.

Trees: Should the tree of your choice not be available in ready-made form as mentioned earlier, and of course if you wish to construct a veritable forest when the cost factor will rear its ugly head, then the following hints for home tree building might prove useful. Strong, stiff twigs form nature's own modules for model trees, and the foliage can be made from sponge which can either be pre-coloured or painted *in situ*. Another more realistic kind of foliage can be bought in hobby

placed over wiring without a plaster base. A fire retarding treatment for polystyrene is available. Less dangerous is a type of foam produced *in situ* by self-flowing polymethanes. One last material that might be used for relatively shallow contours is *papier mâché*. This is basically made from strips of newspaper soaked in water with either wallpaper paste or flour, until a thick paste-like mixture is achieved. The drying time of this mixture is at least 48 hours.

Tunnels: One of the most important parts in the illusion of a model railway is the use of tunnels and, indeed, many of the world's most magnificent model railway systems use tunnels to run trains out of sight and around to the unseen part of the layout of 'fiddleyards' as they are known. Here trains can be taken out of service and generally handled in a way that will not interfere with the realism of the show out front. Tunnels are also vital in the construction of mountain railways where it is necessary to allow trains to climb to great heights without the obviously impossible gradients being on view. Therefore, whatever tunnel is constructed, it should at all times be possible to retrieve a stranded piece of equipment at any part of its length. It is no use having a magnificent express disappear into the Simplon only to require cutting equipment to remove a side of the mountain in order to retrieve it. In this area of scenery, it is almost always necessary for the modeller to construct his own tunnels, although some excellent moulded tunnel facings are available in ready-made form. Earlier we discussed the pre-formed baseboard incorporating its own tunnels and of course these form an exception to the rule. It is always advisable to make a framework for the tunnel, and this will not only give support to the structure, but will tend to ease the problem of dismantling the layout.

shops and this is often pre-coloured. One hint for colouring is to remember the seasons and while conifers remain reasonably constant in their colouring, one has to decide whether it is spring, autumn or winter in colouring the deciduous varieties. Another method of constructing the trunks and branches of trees is to use thin insulated copper or thin galvanised insulation wire having first stripped off the insulation covering. By twisting about a dozen pieces of wire, one can simulate the trunk of a fairly substantial tree, and by progressively using fewer strands of wire the branches as they spread from the main trunk may be created. The whole structure should then be dipped into a bath of either brown or grey quick-drying paint and hung up to dry. Trees are best affixed to the baseboard by drilling a hole in order to 'root' them rather than sticking the trunk to the baseboard which renders their positioning somewhat inflexible. Remember, no model railway is likely to be completely finished before it is taken to pieces and reconstructed; most enthusi-

John B. Porter's HO scale Southern Pacific passenger train crosses the throat at Highfield Yards.

asts find the process of regenerating their model railways continuous.

Mountains: We touched briefly on the construction of hills and mountains through the use of the traditional method of chicken wire and plaster of paris. Another important aid to modelling scenery in recent years has been the tremendous advance in the production of polystyrene. The advantages of this material are twofold. Firstly, it is light and easy to carve and secondly, it can be made into very large structures without any internal formers or supports such as would be necessary to create a large hill or a small mountain with plaster. The one drawback, however, is that care is required when colouring as certain cellulose-based paints attack the fabric of polystyrene and furthermore, there is a slightly higher fire risk with this type of material. Polystyrene should never be

Paint: Most kinds of paint — oil, acrylic, or watercolour can be used for landscaping. In general the paint should be very thin. In the case of oil paint, it should be heavily diluted with turpentine or in the case of watercolour, heavily diluted with water. The effect should be one of staining, rather than heavy painting, except when special effects such as the simulation of water, are required. Do not, as a general rule, use paints with a shiny surface such as enamels or high gloss paint. A look around any landscape will show that there are very few shiny surfaces in nature. Additional aids to natural colouring can be the use of pebbles or small rocks and real sand. Scale is important here and remember when using any of these materials that they should be glued to the layout to avoid their being dislodged, thus interfering with the trackways.

Chapter 5
Metal Kits

In the early days of miniature model railway modelling (and by that one is referring to trains which were meant to run as scenic features and not pull passengers) most model railway equipment was purchased as ready-to-run, and an outline of the history of those trains has been given earlier. As the hobby expanded and enthusiasms became more specialised, it was obvious that the manufacturers could not mass produce every single prototype, however obscure, and still trade profitably. It was in this climate that many small specialised companies grew up, either offering limited runs of locomotives and rolling stock not available from the larger manufacturers or, alternatively, offering similar types but to much higher standards of finish and detail. These offerings obviously suffered the cost penalty, but nonetheless were greatly appreciated by the growing band of model railway enthusiasts intent upon achieving higher levels of realism and specialisation. It was between this area and the mass-produced article that the specialist kit industry grew. Before the Second World War these kits were principally a mixture of brass and white metal castings and often required a great deal of scratch-built detailing in order to achieve the standard necessary. Since the Second World War, the predominant material for most of the components has been white metal, which

is an alloy of zinc and tin. In Japan an even more sophisticated casting process, known as the lost wax process, utilising brass as the main material, was perfected principally for model trains. Some of these were marketed in knocked-down form, although they were mainly of the screw-together variety and did not involve the modeller in any of the finishing techniques required with white metal kits. Several European manufacturers marketed examples of their regular ranges in knocked-down form, but this was usually done to overcome tariff and import duties rather than to provide the modeller with the challenge of building his own model, albeit from pre-formed parts. In fact there were relatively few white metal kits of continental European types, and this may have been due to the fact that there were fewer individual classes of locomotives running in Europe and therefore most of them were likely to be available in ready-to-run form.

To all intents and purposes, the white metal kit now predominates the specialised kit market. One or two companies have tried, with relative degrees of success, to market plastic kits of locomotives, but the chief problem was that it was almost impossible for these to compete with the ready-to-run plastic locomotives which had achieved enormous refinement, particularly in detail and finish. Many

white metal kits were marketed as superstructures only, leaving it to the modeller to purchase a proprietary chassis for which the superstructure was designed. Alternatively, the model maker was required to build his own chassis. Some firms, e.g. Cotswold Models, provided a machined brass chassis with milled coupling rods, but no motor or wheels. The next step from the kit is, of course scratch-built models and this is an area beyond the scope of this book (but nonetheless well served by some excellent books as outlined later). Suffice it to say, however, that for those with the patience and necessary skills, scratch building is the most satisfying of all forms of modelling.

At this stage it might be useful to look at some of the more basic procedures and problems that can arise when attempting to construct a model locomotive kit. For the beginner a wise choice is the body kit designed to fit on to an existing chassis which, since proprietary chassis are now difficult to obtain, will involve converting a locomotive to the modeller's needs. Provided the necessary degree of time and patience are available, the prospective modeller need not possess a high degree of skill to achieve successful completion of the work.

Having purchased the body kit the modeller should ensure that all the parts

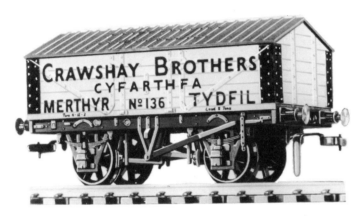

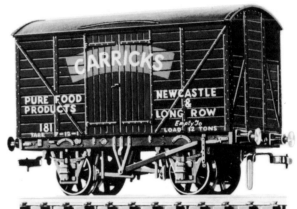

listed and shown on the exploded plan are there and in good condition. Generally, though unfortunately not always, the accompanying instructions will be adequate and simple enough to follow. They should be studied thoroughly and the parts then assembled, as far as possible, in a 'dry run', cleaning off the flash as you go. The 'dry run' is obviously an advantage not only for the practice it provides but also in ensuring that the parts fit together properly and come together in assembled form looking right.

It will be a lucky modeller who does not find at least one part which requires some minor attention: boilers which are slightly out of true in the round but can be gently squeezed back to their correct shape, or cast parts which are slightly distorted but again can be carefully bent to their correct conformation. Of course, if a part is severely malformed or damaged it should be returned to the retailer for replacement.

Different modellers will have different preferences for the order in which they work but since the most significant feature of almost any locomotive model is going to be the boiler, which is often an

Above: A good example of British wagon kits is the range put out by Peco. Originally marketed as Wonderful Wagons *these kits with plastic underframes and brake gear were some of the first to be produced with such fine detail.*

Left: A completed kit of a Johnson 0-4-0T by K's.

integral unit, it would seem sensible to start on its assembly, ensuring that the joins are particularly neatly made where they are visible. Experience will prove that it is a good idea to clean and polish the various parts as you go, always giving units a chance to harden before proceeding to the next stage. Not all parts are going to fit together simply without some means of support while they are positioned and when the fixative chosen — be it epoxy or cyanoacrylatic adhesive or solder — is hardening. Clips, adhesive tape and Blu-tak are all useful aids here and individual ingenuity will produce others.

The soldering or gluing processes are dealt with below but other aids which are worth mentioning here are two pairs of pliers, a sound flat working surface, a small woodwork vice, a drill (No 74 in a pin chuck should meet most needs), a filler such as car body putty, epoxy resin, fine-grade Polyfilla etc, a small needle file, a set square to ensure, for example, that vent pipes and chimneys are vertical, and a toothbrush and scouring powder. Remember, too, that number and name plates will need to be ordered from specialist engravers and that there is likely to be a wait before they are delivered. A woodwork vice can be used gently to squeeze that misshapen boiler back into the perfect round. The drill is required to make the holes for smaller fittings and if the previously mentioned No 74 bit does not provide a large enough hole, the needle file can be used for opening up to the correct size. One particular use for the pliers is in straightening the wire provided for handrails, holding one end in the vice and the other in the pliers and pulling steadily to remove bends and kinks. (An even better method is to roll the wire between two pieces of flat board.) The toothbrush and scouring powder are used when the whole model is assembled to give it an overall scrub, followed by a thorough clean in mild detergent water to prepare it for painting.

If the modeller decides to use an adhesive he should beware not to make use of any of the quick-drying varieties since these do not provide sufficient time to make final adjustments or rectify errors.

The principal advantage of soldering is that it is possible to unstick a previously soldered joint, while the chief disadvantage is that, without experience, it is easy to melt the castings at the points at which they are being soldered. Fortunately, a solder with a low melting point and designed specifically for use with white metal kits is available.

If one or two precautions are taken, soldering need not be too daunting a prospect. For example: use a soldering iron with a small bit, the tip of which can be placed exactly where required; hold the tip over the point to be soldered and do not let it wander; ensure that the iron, the flux and the parts to be soldered are really clean and with emery lightly rub down the white metal parts to be soldered at the points where they are to be joined. The solder should be cut into easily managed lengths or even into the tiny amounts required for each join.

Hold the two parts to be soldered in position and apply a very small amount of flux. Then place the end of the solder on the flux (or, if the tiny piece is being used, drop it on to the flux) and apply the tip of the iron to the solder — not to the two parts to be joined but as close to them as possible. The solder will melt within one or two seconds, flow freely and conduct its heat to the two parts to form the joint. If a white metal casting has to be joined to a brass part, first tin the piece of brass at the point of the join, place it in position and put on the flux. The tip of the iron should be applied to the brass — not to the white metal — and the tinning will flow to form the joint as before.

The final and most important stage of the whole model is that of painting. Whatever the final colour scheme, the model should first be sprayed or painted with a primer, care being taken at this stage not to handle the model with bare hands. Whether the final livery is hand-painted or sprayed will depend on the modeller's equipment, but one is bound to say that it is very difficult to compete with the finishes that can be achieved with today's sophisticated spray guns.

The final and most difficult addition to the finish of the model locomotive is the lining and here one can, to an extent, opt out of the problem by using one of the many excellent lining transfers that are available, or alternatively hand line or spray, using appropriate masking materials available for this purpose. In the case of lining on certain coach kits, the problem is often overcome by the lining having been photo-engraved on to the piece parts. For the talented few unaided hand lining is the only answer and for some of the aids to hand lining the reader is referred to *The Complete Car Modeller* by Gerald A. Wingrove.

Above, centre right and bottom right: These three old-time box cars were assembled by Emery J. Gulash from kits manufactured by Stewart-Lundhac of North Hollywood, California. They are O gauge ¼-inch scale.

Top right: The components of the Thomas 2-8-0 consolidation kit in process of assembly.

Below: An American post-war manufacturer, Thomas Industries had an early period 2-8-0 kit in O gauge ¼-in scale.

Chapter 6
MODEL TRAIN
COLLECTING

Perhaps one of the most surprising developments in the post-war period has been the rise in the popularity of collecting vintage toy and model trains. It would appear that as prices escalate so more people are drawn into the field and at the same time the dates at which model railway items become collectable advance accordingly. The hobby really originated in America as early as 1936 when a magazine devoted to tinplate enthusiasts, called *Model Railroaders' Digest* was launched. Although there may have been isolated collectors in Europe at this time there is little evidence of their joining together in an effort to publish material or otherwise disseminate and exchange information. As with so many things at this time, much valuable information and material may have been lost to posterity.

One of the pioneer thinkers in this hobby was undoubtedly Louis Hertz who not only became a major contributor to *Model Railroaders' Digest*, but later wrote two of the 'bibles' of the hobby, *Riding The Tinplate Rails* and *Collecting Model Trains*, to which reference is made later.

Having established *where* model train collecting started, perhaps we can have a look at *why*. If we start with the purest motive, and indeed initially this may be a prime motive for most collectors, i.e. that of nostalgia, then at least this presents a fairly understandable reason to surround oneself with one or two relics of youth. Indeed it may even take the form of wishing to acquire model trains which one did *not* have the opportunity or the means to possess in earlier days.

It was once fairly simple to define an antique in that it was usually an object that was at least one hundred years old, but now the word antique is almost irrelevant as objects can become collectable and given antique status within years rather than centuries of their obsolescence. This is particularly relevant when collecting model trains as the desirability factor has as much to do with value as absolute age or even rarity. The word value would have to creep in sooner or later, so let us deal with it here. Whereas the original motive for collecting anything may be totally divorced from its monetary value, if the collector continues beyond perhaps a handful of objects, he becomes aware of the changing values of, in this case, the trains he is buying. Within a short time of being initiated into this hobby, people mention values that they would have deemed ridiculous when they first decided to collect. Whereas only a few years ago people would tend to ignore the effect of inflation, there are few today in any field who do not bring this into the equation, therefore, something purchased in, say, 1972 which has now doubled in value is not quite as surprising as it would seem

at first sight if one deducts the inflation factor, about 6 × 15% for the UK. Therefore, one must make the decision that collecting model trains is at least enjoyable, for the most miserable collector is the one who has no empathy towards the subject matter of his collection, i.e. those terrible people who collect silver and put it in vaults and then earnestly discuss its aesthetic value. Thus, whether desirable or not the collection of model trains, like other relatively new collectables has the characteristic of both enjoyment and investment. The absolute purist can, of course, divorce the investment aspect from his mind, but sooner or later he or his dependants will either reap the benefit or loss of the investment factor. Some collections even start for more amusing reasons, in that the collector is a failed model railway operator, i.e. somebody who becomes so intrigued with buying locomotives and rolling stock that he either has no room or money left to build the railway.

Whatever the reason, having taken the decision to allocate space to a model train collection, thought then needs to be given to the scope and nature of the collection. Most collectors' long term experience is that more is seldom better, other than for people who have unlimited resources and space. Discrimination, as in many aspects of life, is essential if one is to derive any element of enjoyment from a model train collection. One will usually find that even the largest and wealthiest collectors cannot acquire it all, and those who have tried to go down this road have frequently become frustrated in that their collections become a liability and no longer something of pleasure. It can also lead to a worse symptom, that of obsession, when the collection craze seems to assume greater importance than any other single factor in the collector's life. Notwithstanding that the collector may have three examples of a particular locomotive, he feels obsessed to have a fourth or even a fifth or however many present themselves. There is, of course the collector of variations, and this in model trains can also lead to large numbers of virtually identical items being acquired. This is fine if the collector restrains himself to one type or even a narrow period, but if his taste extends over a large period and many types, an extraordinary amount of space must be made available. So, the general advice to the newcomer is collect what you enjoy, and in today's conditions, what you can afford. If you happen to enjoy very expensive things, i.e. Marklin Cock O' The North locomotives or Crocodiles, then take the decision fairly early on to collect just a few things of high quality. However assuming that your tastes are less

exotic, the best discipline is to collect the products of just one manufacturer or a particular gauge or period. One of the finest private collections of toys in the world, not exclusively trains, is confined to mint examples of toys produced before 1914. You may say this leaves the field wide open, but in reality perhaps only one or two items worthy of inclusion within such a strictly defined collection come to light each year, and therefore the collection is self-regulating. For the English collector, Hornby is a classic example of one collectable product, and indeed the Hornby Railway Collectors Association is comprised of some 500 people of like interest. Even within collecting Hornby one can restrict oneself to

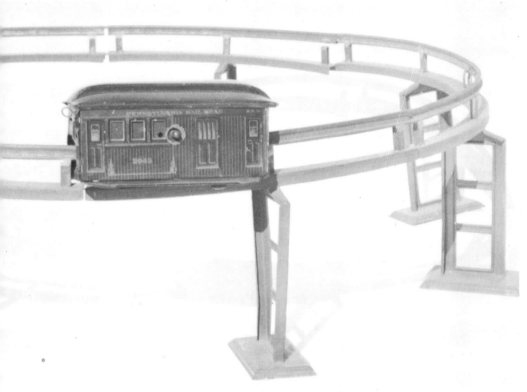

boxed or mint items only. It is however more difficult in this particular case to restrict oneself to periods, because of course the Hornby gauge O period effectively only spanned some twenty years. In America there are probably more specialised collectors of Lionel equipment than any other and in this case the natural division is between standard gauge and O gauge.

At this stage one should perhaps point out the generally accepted meaning of the terms vintage and tinplate. Vintage denotes some age, and for all practical purposes model trains produced up to the Second World War may now be classed as vintage. 'Tinplate' was initially an American expression and really it refers

Top: Marescot of France were the pioneers of gauge O fine scale modelling in the late 1920s and this superb Etat Pacific and cars illustrate that firm's supremacy at that time.

Above: While many transport designers experimented with monorail systems, the toymakers often produced their own creations. In this illustration the very rare Marklin clockwork monorail for the American market is shown. Basically the car is a converted O gauge Pennsylvania RR baggage car and is thought to have been produced prior to the First World War, although not catalogued until thereafter.

less to the materials used in the manufacture of a particular train and more to its coarse scale and toy-like qualities, so much a feature of early commercial railways. Once again most commercially made model railway equipment made up to the Second World War would fall within this definition, although there are some exotic exceptions such as the near scale trains of Marescot and Founereau of France and in England, J. S. Beeson and to a lesser degree Leeds Model Company and Edward Exley's products. However, sub-areas in collecting interests can be found among those people who only collect accessories. Indeed those who have specialised particularly in pre-First World War stations and lineside accessories will be reaping a rich harvest as for many years these were the things that were given away with the rolling stock and were not regarded as having any intrinsic merit as single items.

Having decided what to collect — and being realistic, of course, few people stick rigidly to their original game plans — the next question arises as to where to come across the equipment. Fifteen or twenty years ago suitably worded advertisements in the model railway press or even the national newspapers would bring forth a highly credible rate of response, particularly as up to that time few people, other than the committed collector, took the field of collecting model trains seriously. Some shrewd hobby shop owners, particularly in the United States, were happy to exchange modern HO equipment for vintage trains; new lamps for old! But that was all some time ago and the situation has considerably changed today. The evidence of the growth of the hobby may be seen in the fact that the Train Collectors' Association of America, the TCA, has some 15,000 members and this obviously only reflects a propor-

tion of the actual number of people interested in the study and collection of vintage railway equipment. Returning to the problem of locating equipment today, it is fair to say that of the total remaining model railway equipment manufactured up to 1939, the largest proportion is in the hands of known collectors and in some instances has probably been through the hands of many collectors since its original appearance on the market. Thus equipment held in this way can be secured by arranging exchanges — which as any veteran collector will know sometimes involves sessions lasting far into the night. There is always the natural process of collectors either giving up or changing the content of their collection or merely succumbing to Anno Domini, and in this case it may be possible for the new collector to start his collection with a cash acquisition, either direct from the collector or via one of the many public auctions which regularly include model trains. Of course the collector may sell or exchange with a known dealer, normally operating a shop specialising in this type of item. Far more intriguing from the collector's point of view is the opportunity to buy equipment from a non-collector who in many instances represents the original owner. It is here that the real finds occur, however, it is also in this area that a high degree of honesty is required as in many instances this type of sale is through need, possibly on the loss of a husband, and little pleasure should be gained from buying an item worth, say £100 for £10. (If however one buys a bargain at public auction it is an entirely different matter and probably the fault of the auction.) This is a difficult area, but the general approach should be one of exercising fairness and consideration. For this purpose, of course, a collector advertising in trade journals or local newspapers is likely to be brought into contact with private, non-collectors. Among collectors the Swap Meet and Flea Market have now become regular

sources of supply, but it is often a question of who can arrive first rather than any other factor. Individual items have been known to change hands two or three times during a day at these meets. In America, the TCA train meet at York, Pennsylvania, has reached colossal proportions, reflecting the enthusiasm and following of this fascinating hobby.

Now we will consider the matter of the condition of the equipment. In America there is a system for defining, mint, fair, reasonable or poor, and members of the TCA are obliged to adhere strictly to this star system when advertising or describing items that may be purchased unseen. However, for the average collector the question of appraising condition is more likely to rest on his knowledge of what the original looked like. It is obvious that the ideal is a piece of equipment in mint condition, wrapped in its original box. While items such as these still come to light, they are very much the exception and, indeed any item that appears to be mint, but has certain key replacement parts (or where the mechanism appears to have had a considerable amount of wear compared to the rest of the body) should arouse some natural suspicion on the part of the intending purchaser. The art of restoration is very

advanced today and indeed in America virtually any part of a vintage Lionel train can be acquired off the shelf, brand new, and the unwary new collector can hardly distinguish this from the original. Care at this end of the market is obviously necessary as it goes without saying that mint original items, leaving aside their desirability, have a considerable premium in value alone when compared with their less well-maintained counterparts. At the other end of the scale, there is the matter of the item that is in extremely bad condition with parts missing and the paintwork badly damaged. If one has a general rule concerning restorations then it is *don't*. Or in a more qualified form don't unless you know exactly what the original looked like. There is little doubt that a badly restored model train or piece of rolling stock has even less value than an equivalent item in poor condition. As with an old master, the original paintwork is far more precious than any new application and every effort should be made to retain the original by diligent cleaning. Furthermore one must learn to live with the item in that form until a better example comes to light. Obviously the question of restoration either in whole or part can only apply to those items that were originally painted or enamelled and if one is faced with an original lithographed item which is badly scratched, then restoration is virtually impossible. Although touching in of some of the blemishes can sometimes be successful retouching lithographed items can rarely be totally disguised. Having made these remarks it is obvious that anything in even average condition should not be meddled with other than by diligent cleaning. It is always worthwhile when coming across a piece of model railway equipment that appears to have been completely overpainted to very carefully carry out some tests with light solutions of paint stripper in order to see whether the original livery exists beneath the overpaint. It must be stressed that only very light solutions of solvent should be used as there is a tendency to remove not only the offending overpaint, but also the precious original livery. Although it is undesirable to restore equipment in terms of paintwork, this does not, of course apply quite as rigorously to other parts. With present-day casting techniques most metal objects are reproducible and few would argue that a coach without wheels or a locomotive without a chimney is desirable, providing the replacement part can be manufactured by somebody with a first hand knowledge of the original. Reproduction pressed metal parts are however somewhat less available.

Now we come again to the slightly sensitive question of value. Value in model trains as in many other areas of collecting is based on two main factors, desirability (which includes the supply and demand factor) and condition. Determining the latter is relatively easy in that by reference to catalogues and, even better, the actual object in a fellow collector's collection, the relative condition can be determined with some degree of accuracy. It is here that the age is a subsidiary factor, because, of course, one would expect a higher standard of original appearance from a later item than an earlier one. Indeed an earlier item may be in virtually original condition, but the paint may have crazed purely through the passage of time, this condition being relative. However there have been outstanding examples of model trains from the turn of the century coming to light in the virtually mint condition in which they were purchased by the original owners. Desirability can be broken down into several subsidiary factors, foremost of which is *who* desires the particular item. This may at first sight appear flippant, but is highly relevant to the price that anybody pays for anything, other than the absolute necessities of life which everybody requires. Here the factor of rarity comes into play, because it is usually the case that an item which is rare and therefore in few collections will have a greater relative value than an item of similar size and period, in more plentiful supply. The relative affluence coupled with the number of people collecting a particular make has a great bearing on the value of that item. Rarity alone does not create high value as, for instance, a very rare item by an obscure manufacturer collected by very few people may not be anywhere near as valuable or desirable as a relatively commonplace item collected by a large group of people. Age is not an absolute criteria either in the value of a model train and it would be fair to say at the present time that examples from the 1920s and 1930s are, as a general rule, more valuable than those from most earlier periods. This state of affairs may be due to nostalgia which leads collectors to pay a premium for items which represent railways with which they were vaguely familiar and formed part of their lifetime's experience. As another general rule of thumb, the value of a 'good big one' will always be more than a 'good little one'! This applies to gauge and scale as well as to individual types within a particular gauge. Thus a Pacific locomotive in O gauge will almost certainly be more valuable than, say an 0-6-0 tank engine, unless the latter displays some extremely rare feature or happens to be the one item missing from a very large collection. Thus, as you will see, desirability is an amalgam of collectors' demands, but it has now become highly relevant in that whereas in the past the value of secondhand vintage trains was invariably less than their replacement value. Today this is certainly not the case, and the collector is paying a considerable premium for the desirability or emotional factor.

The scope of model train collecting is by no means confined to collecting vintage trains, i.e. those manufactured up to 1939. All the criteria discussed above apply equally to collections of post-war scale models. For instance collectors of Japanese brass locomotives in either HO or OO or of Pochers superb post-war HO plastic and metal range know all about how many were made, and when, and which are the *right* ones. To the layman it is probably easier to understand the value of, for example, a KTM O gauge Japanese brass Big Boy than a Lionel Blue Comet locomotive and unless one has a real feeling for the rather more crude and toylike vintage trains, a newcomer should confine himself to models that seem to represent good value. Taking this argument one stage further, there is, of course, no reason at all why plastic trains should not become the highly sought after collectables of the future and indeed that process has already begun. In some instances it has gone rather too far in that major manufacturers, such as Lionel are actually producing limited runs of trains as collectors' editions. One is not at all certain that this artificial collectability which bears a certain similarity to the medal collecting syndrome is founded on any real intrinsic merit or value other than the artificial 'rarity' factor. Ironically, the rarest and most desirable collectables are those which were complete or partial commercial failures in their contemporary days and marvellous white elephants such as Marklin's Rheinuferbahn of the 1930s and Schoenner's PLM Coup Vent are enthusiastically sought today.

The last word on collecting model railways is display, and here one returns to the original reason for collecting, namely enjoyment. Unless the collection is displayed in a manner in which it can be enjoyed, it might as well be in the vault along with the Georgian silver! There are two schools of thought concerning the display of a model train collection. One dictates that you put every conceivable item you own on show and the the other suggests that only part of a large collection can be digested at any one time and, therefore, only a relatively small display should be made in order that items can be regularly rotated. Thus your friends and/or fellow collectors may see something different each time they call. The determining factor is obviously space, and anybody fortunate enough to have sufficient space to create a private museum would probably be in a position to display most of his collection in a pleasing and aesthetic way. If the space available is at a premium, then one should show only as much as will provide real enjoyment without spoiling the display by overcrowding and without giving the visitor indigestion. Probably the ideal way of exhibiting vintage trains is to have them on a working vintage layout with all the accessories of the period. This is an aim that most collectors strive towards after several years of static display and the thought of having one's collection in a living form with all the clatter, headlights and that marvellous smell of ozone is the ultimate reward.

Most collectors will find that as they progress they are all the while upgrading the quality of the things they have, and in many instances actually reducing the size of their collection as the level of their taste reaches for greater heights. One can rationalise this situation to a point where the collection can reduce to one classic train set in totally original condition, sitting resplendent in its original box. Like the Holy Grail few people will achieve the ultimate in their field of collecting, but then the pursuit is almost as interesting as the goal.

Chapter 7
PHOTOGRAPHY

Top left inset: Realism at the station. Ken Ball's Fraddon station: the buildings and road vehicles are scratch built.

Above: Snow scene — more Midland Railway realism, this time a scene constructed by Ken Ball and Brian Monaghan.

Having completed his layout — if any layout can ever be said to be truly complete — many a modeller may well want to record his success photographically both *in toto* and, by close-up work, in part.

Photographing a model railway layout or a section of it is an art in itself. It is a relatively simple matter to take static shots of a particular locomotive or piece of rolling stock for the purpose of showing it in detail *as a model*. It is entirely another and more difficult matter to continue the sense of realism which has been brought to the modelling into the finished photograph.

However realistic a layout or its component parts may appear in their actuality, lack of care in setting up and taking the photograph can reduce the whole thing to a static flatness and result in a print which positively screams 'model!' at you; rocks which look real enough on a layout shout 'cork bark' from the emulsion and waving grass whispers 'sawdust'.

The art of successful model photography is the art of deception. The camera which never lies can, in fact, be a great ally in putting the finishing touches to realism. For a start — assuming the right camera angles and distance from the subject are selected — life-size background objects which immediately 'minify' a model can be cut out so that the print shows only the area of a model in which everything is to scale. The camera thus deceives the eye, which in turn deceives the mind into accepting that one is not looking at a miniature train but at the real thing.

One of the most important factors which can either contribute to a successful photograph or totally spoil it is lighting. If one is dealing with an outdoor layout there should be no great problem since natural light is best so long as it is not too harsh. A glaring midsummer sun, for example, will tend to harden outlines and create shadows which, photographically, are too dense. Remember always to check that neither the photographer nor the camera is throwing a shadow across the subject area. Shadows can be relieved both out of doors and inside by using reflective material to direct light on to them. However, a word of caution here: silver cooking foil can be used successfully for this purpose but if a strong light source is being used, beware of too many wrinkles in the foil since these will tend to give a dappled effect in the reflected light.

It is possible to use flash either singly or in relay but it is generally best to direct the flash gun away from the central subject of the photograph and not to have it too close to it. An advantage of using more than one flash gun is that one can be used to 'bounce' light indirectly on to

the subject area to give a softer effect or to avoid some shadowing by creating a form of back lighting. Always remove the flash gun from the camera and connect the two with an extension lead. Do not try to use the camera by holding it in the hands; either place it on the layout or use a rigid support such as a tripod. As a further aid to avoiding camera shake (which is a problem when working at the necessarily slow speeds), do not use the shutter release button but a flexible cable shutter release. Ideally this should be at least 12 inches (0.3 m) long to facilitate easier operation if the camera has to be placed in a difficult position.

If artificial light is necessary — and it almost certainly will be when working indoors — 500 watt photoflood lamps are an excellent source, always bearing in mind that they have only a short working life. The lamps give off a high density of light but burn out in about two hours and so should not be left on unnecessarily — one more reason for ensuring that one is entirely satisfied with the camera positioning and with exactly what area the lens will be covering.

The 500 watt photofloods can be used quite close to the subject to be photographed (preferably with reflectors) but it should be noted that this will tend to produce a concentration of light on the point at which they are directed but a rapid falling off in intensity within a short radius. There is, therefore, a danger that the edges of the scene will be poorly exposed.

Nowadays the most convenient camera to use for model photography would certainly seem to be one of the many small, compact 35 mm makes. These have all the advantages of being equipped with short focus lenses and, because of their size, they can be placed in positions which would be inaccessible to larger cameras.

A camera which has a fairly short focal length giving a good depth of focus is necessary. The ideal would probably be a lens of 30 mm focal length or even less, but the average camera is more likely to have a lens of between 38 and 50 mm with which it will not be possible to get quite as close to the subject. Even so, perfectly satisfactory results can still be obtained. Another point of importance is that the camera will need to have a good aperture range, particularly at the smaller stop end of the scale since the smaller the aperture, the greater the depth of focus obtainable (and the better lighting needed). The focal length of a lens is usually marked on it as '1:2.8/38' or with the '1:28' stamped in one position and '38 mm' or whatever the focal length of the lens is, marked elsewhere. The first figure simply means that the maximum aperture is f2.8. In fact it is extreme-

ly unlikely that such a wide aperture would be used for this type of work. Instead, one is likely to be working at a maximum of f14 down to the minimum, if one's camera has it, of f32. Thus one will therefore be using slow shutter speeds — sometimes of several seconds duration.

A very considerable advantage is to be gained by using a single lens reflex camera because in the viewfinder the photographer will see the exact scene area he is photographing. Without the benefit of a single lens reflex you will need to carry out a little experimenting to discover how closely the scene in the viewfinder of your camera corresponds with that which will be pictured on the film. There will certainly be a difference between the two as will be discovered by opening the back of the camera, placing a piece of tracing paper as a screen in the position normally occupied by the film and setting the shutter on time, or on 'bulb' and holding it open. The scene which is projected on to the paper will be that which will appear on the film and it can be compared with the view seen through the viewfinder. Since the centre of the viewfinder is not in the same position as the centre of the lens — the viewfinder will be left or right and above the lens — there will be a difference between the two 'pictures' seen. Having noted that difference it is no great problem to select through the viewfinder the scene

Above: Alistair *and train at Glenmuir – a lonely spot on P. D. Hancock's 4 mm scale Craig & Mertonford Light Railway. The coaches are American style vehicles built from Kemtron photo-engraved brass sides. The plume of smoke from* Alistair's *chimney is a not altogether successful attempt at 'trick' photography: as the photographer says, it would have looked better had the piece of cotton wool used to represent the smoke been moved around a bit more during the time exposure required to take the photograph.*

one wishes to photograph and then move the camera the few centimetres left or right and up to bring the centre of the lens into the position which was occupied by the viewfinder.

To carry out this experiment it will be necessary to have the aperture wide open to admit as much light as possible and it will be noticed that the scene projected on to the tracing paper shows very little depth of focus. However, stopping down the aperture increases the depth of focus and this should be done after one has selected the central feature of the proposed picture and focused upon it. It will then be found that the depth of focus extends over probably two to five inches (5 to 12.7 cm). The fact that the background tends to be out-of-focus actually adds to the realism of the scene, so long as the primary object of the picture is sharp.

If the camera does not focus below 12 inches (0.3 m), it will be necessary to use a close-up lens, the choice of which depends to a great extent on the scale of the models being photographed. For example, a No 3 or even a No 2 lens should be adequate for taking shots of OO and HO gauge and the American-inspired TT gauge, while a No 1 could be employed for O gauge.

As a rough guide to the capabilities of the various close-up lenses mentioned the following tables are of use.

No 3	Camera setting	Lens to subject
	3 ft (0.91 m)	9.5 in (24.1 cm)
	4 ft (1.22 m)	10.5 in (26.6 cm)
	5 ft (1.52 m)	10.75 in (27.3 cm)
	6 ft (1.83 m)	11.00 in (27.9 cm)
	8 ft (2.43 m)	11.5 in (29.1 cm)
	12 ft (3.66 m)	12.00 in (30.4 cm)
	25 ft (7.62 m)	12.5 in (31.7 cm)
	Infinity	13.00 in (33.0 cm)

No 2	Camera setting	Lens to subject
	3 ft (0.91 m)	12.75 in (32.4 cm)
	4 ft (1.22 m)	14.00 in (35.5 cm)
	5 ft (1.52 m)	14.75 in (37.4 cm)
	6 ft (1.83 m)	15.5 in (39.3 cm)
	7 ft (2.13 m)	16.00 in (40.6 cm)
	12 ft (3.66 m)	17.25 in (43.8 cm)
	15 ft (4.57 m)	17.75 in (45.1 cm)
	20 ft (6.10 m)	18.25 in (46.3 cm)
	Infinity	19.75 in (50.1 cm)

No 1	Camera setting	Lens to subject
	3 ft (0.91 m)	18.5 in (46.9 cm)
	4 ft (1.22 m)	21.75 in (55.2 cm)
	5 ft (1.52 m)	23.75 in (60.3 cm)
	6 ft (1.83 m)	25.50 in (64.7 cm)
	7 ft (2.13 m)	27.75 in (70.4 cm)
	12 ft (3.66 m)	30.00 in (76.1 cm)
	15 ft (4.57 m)	32.25 in (81.9 cm)
	20 ft (6.10 m)	34.00 in (86.3 cm)
	Infinity	39.25 in (99.6 cm)

A final point worth considering is that model photography is possibly the hardest task master for the modeller in that close-up still photographs pick out faults.

Left: Realism on the narrow gauge — a scene on the Quarry layout of H. Halsall using N gauge 9 mm track and 4 mm scale rolling stock (OOn9).

Above: Realism in N gauge — the Gransmoor Castle layout of the Manchester Model Railway Society.

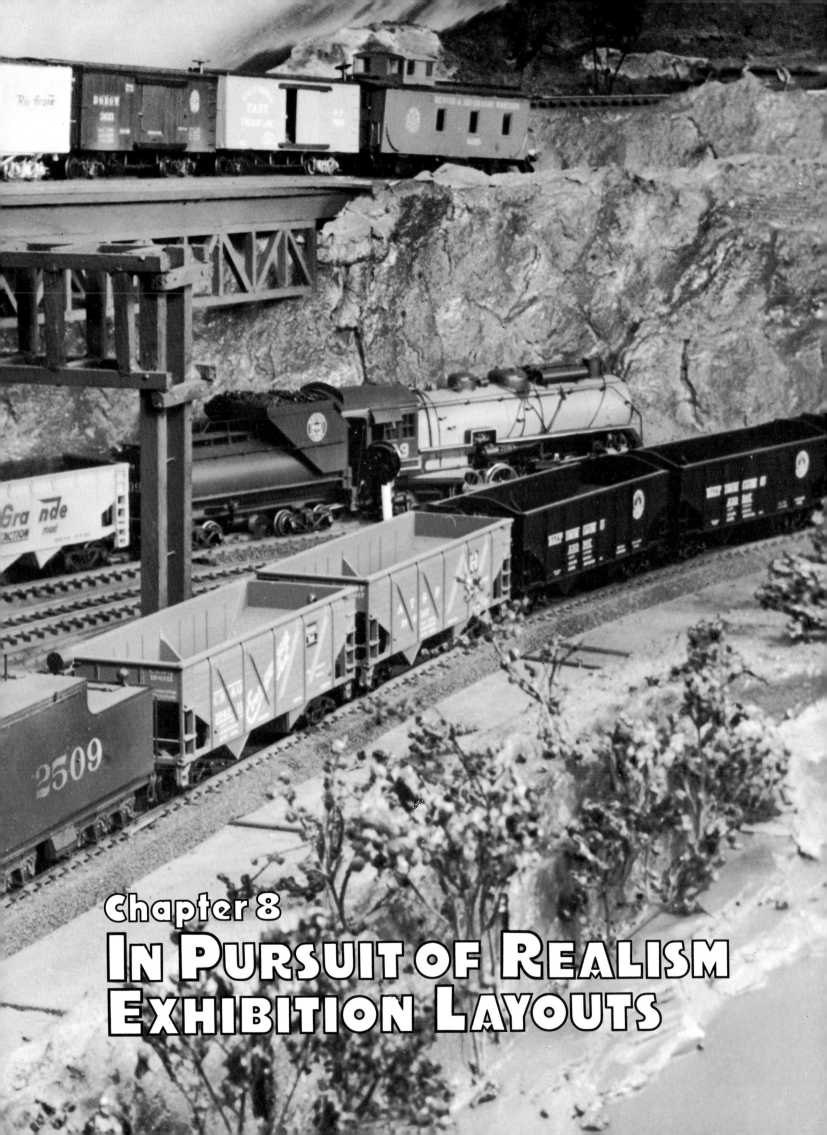

Chapter 8
In Pursuit of Realism
Exhibition Layouts

Pendon Museum's Great Western Railway Saint Class 4-6-0 No 2921 Saint Dunstan heads a period train of clerestorey coaches and vans over a replica Brunel wooden viaduct. The layout is EM gauge, 4 mm fine scale.

The ultimate goal for every serious modeller should always be to achieve a sense of realism in the finished work, and this is all the more so if a particular project involves different branches of modelling. If, for example, a model locomotive and its attendant stock are to be set in a model landscape the whole effect may be ruined if, however perfect the railway side of things may be, the countryside in which it travels does not look right, is out of perspective or scale, or is either too modern or too old. There is possibly no better way of gaining inspiration than by seeing some of the really great models which are on show and discovering how they were constructed and what tricks of the trade were used to achieve that sense of realism, without which they would not have become famous. There are, of course, many models on display, covering every gauge and a wide variety of periods and styles. It would be impossible to cover

adequately even a fraction of them here but it is, nonetheless, worth considering some of the best as an indication of what they contain and of what can be achieved.

The old villages of England which he considered in danger of being unrecognisably renovated were the inspiration for Roye England to begin work on a model which has become world famous as the Pendon Museum at Long Wittenham, Berkshire, near Wallingford and Oxford.

He arrived in Britain from Australia in the 1930s and fell in love with the Great Western Railway and with the thatched villages. He already had a third love — modelling. Combining the three he was eventually able to begin work on constructing the model which he determined would be 'a study in topography, aiming to create a countryside where the railways and roads, the hill-set village, even the work of the farms in progress will form a natural part of the rural setting which surrounds them'. It was to be a model *par excellence*, setting new standards of realism and perpetuating an England that was fast disappearing.

The period he chose to represent was, in itself, an interesting one. He believed

that the years from 1923 to 1937 were the best inter-war years and a time in which the individuality which preceded the grouping days could still be seen and the railways had matured. Very soon after this time great railway changes were to sweep away features of the 1930s, quickly in the urban areas but more insidiously in the country. Today very little remains of those days except in photographs or the realism of models such as Pendon.

In pursuit of his dream Roye England travelled many thousands of miles about the country, mostly by bicycle, photographing specific buildings, streets or landscapes and taking careful note of colours, textures and any peculiar features. He knew that to achieve the superlative standards which he was setting was beyond the capabilities of one man and he gathered together a team of dedicated people who had more than just enthusiasm to offer. His original team included people such as Guy Williams, already a successful locomotive modeller, Ken Budd, for coach building, Paul King for track work and control, Jim Arnold for scenery, Stewart Hine for electronics. England himself was already working on the architectural details when, in 1961, the Pendon Museum Trust Ltd, a non-profit-making company registered as a charity, came into being. Together, the team, which later rose to over 50 workers, modellers, helpers and members, set

about making the model with near-perfection as their goal and always bearing in mind the thought that they were not only building for themselves but also for visitors. Hence the design was laid down with the idea that the viewer should be able to see as much detail as possible and without close scrutiny of the model ruining the effect.

The Pendon model, built to a scale of 4 mm to the foot (1:76) includes a moorland scene 46 feet long and featuring a tunnel opening on to a 16-tier Brunel timber viaduct, the Vale of White Horse, some 70 feet long, and the model village, Pendon Parva, with its cottages, chapel and farm.

The railway is built to 18 mm gauge fine scale and includes a superb collection of locomotives and stock covering every type of train from express to slow-moving goods. A popular feature is the lighted train with its fully-fitted interior, complete with passengers and staff in fine detail (the ticket collector even wears a tiny carnation buttonhole!). The sense of realism has been achieved as a result of the meticulous attention to detail and the modelling methods which have been employed.

One of Roye England's superb hand-crafted buildings on display at Pendon Museum.

Roye England uses white pasteboard 0.5 mm to 0.75 mm thick almost exclusively for his architectural work. His preference is for white PVA adhesive. Walls are made in one piece, the board being V-grooved at the back to allow folding for corners. Before folding, the walls are scored, using a blunt point, with marks to represent the type of finish — stones are done in freehand, bricks require ruled lines — and are then completely covered in mortar-coloured watercolour. This is followed by the detailed and meticulous painting of the individual bricks or stones. Attention is paid to the variety of colours which can be found in any stone or brick surface and this often requires more than one coat to give the correct final effect. A useful tip is that the walls are always extended some 30 mm below ground level and this provides a finger hold which is not on the water-colouring. In addition, if a building is to be sited on sloping ground this extra depth to the walls means that the ground can be added at the chosen level and

angle without any problem, so that the building sits on buried foundations.

Frames of windows, which extend behind the walls to give the impression of depth, are made either from strips of thin card or paper and glazing bars are made from slivers of card or from No 60 cotton which is dipped in water colour, dried and then stretched over the frame. The glazing is with mica. Whether or not they are to be visible, floors and walls are always put in to provide the structure with extra rigidity.

Furniture is usually constructed from card about 0.3 mm thick and appropriately coloured while paper tissue is used to represent fabrics such as tablecloths. Tissue is also used for flower petals and leaves. A double-thickness tissue is painted on both sides and then allowed to dry, whereupon it becomes strong and can be cut or bent easily.

Interior lighting is by torch bulbs concealed in shafts made from card from which the bulb can be withdrawn by its lead for replacement. It is important to place the shaft with care, not only to ensure that the bulb cannot be seen but also to provide the correct lighting effect.

As with every other feature, great care

is taken in constructing the roofs of the buildings, whether they are of slate, stone, tile or thatch. First, card partitions are placed in the positions which would normally be occupied by rafters; then an under-roof made from card is put on, followed by the final outer covering. To achieve a sagging effect the under-roof card is replaced by strips of paper run loosely over the 'rafters' and the tiles or slates are laid on these. The tiles are made from 0.3 mm card and painted separately, slates are made from paper and stone tiles from thicker card which is cut with slightly irregular edges.

For thatching plumbers' hemp (tow) is used, and bundles of it are laid in similar fashion to that used by real thatchers, working from the lower edge of the roof upwards and trimming with curved scissors held vertically. Wire or linen thread pegged with bent entomological pins is used for runners and the thatched roof is weathered with slightly diluted Humbrol paint. At one time Roye England used human hair for thatching but he finds the tow easier to use and to obtain.

The ground contours are constructed from a boxwork of card cut to the appropriate lines and with mutton cloth or butter muslin stretched over. A mix of Polyfilla and sawdust is laid on this surface to provide strength and texture. When this is well set the scenery is added, by using mainly matt oil paints.

Paper tissue is used again to make trees. Twisted copper wire forms the trunk and is spread in appropriate thicknesses for branches; this 'skeleton' is then painted with matt Humbrol and wrapped in the tissue while still wet. The tissue absorbs the paint and as it dries takes on the appearance of bark. The upper foliage of trees depends upon their type: minced rubber sponge is satisfactory for oak trees, for example, and sawdust is used for elms. Under foliage is usually made from rubberised horsehair. The finished tree is spray-painted. Undergrowth, shrubs, bushes and small vegetation, flowers and vegetables can all be made from rubberised horsehair, sponge rubber, lichen, moss, paper tissue and sawdust. Flower stems are fashioned by Roye England from hair, cat's whiskers, cotton or small feathers.

The team at Pendon is constantly searching for new materials — or for old materials which can be successfully adapted to a new use.

Also on view at Pendon Museum is the Madder Valley model which forms a suitable memorial to its creator, John Ahern, one of the world's pioneer modellers. Ahern, a man of considerable artistic and constructional skills and of imagination, began building his model railway in 1937, working almost entirely from scratch and steadily enlarging the project to include not only the railway layout but also a seaport town and harbour, countryside and two villages. The whole includes models of real buildings which its creator had seen in the country and the setting covers the 1920–30 period. Its area is some 17 feet by 10 feet yet, despite the amount of detail which it contains, there is no sense of overcrowding.

John Ahern worked at the construction of his Madder Valley over 25 years, on and off, until his death in 1962. At that time part of the model had been dismantled for further alterations and the rest had been cut into sections and stored when he moved house. Not long after his death his widow offered Madder Valley to Pendon Museum on permanent loan. It was readily accepted and reassembled, but when the old museum building was demolished and the new took its place, the Valley again had to be stored. On its re-erection it was altered from its original U-shape to an L-shape to give better viewing facilities.

The Valley was evolved over the quarter of a century during which many changes were made by John Ahern, who frequently shifted features in a search for the best possible scenic effects. The railway line itself runs close to the River Madder, starting from the terminal in Gammon Magna, the village on high ground with a curving main street running uphill and a castle. From the station the line runs down the valley, through a rock tunnel carved out of the foothills of the Madderhorn. A low-level branch line from Gammon End Halt runs parallel to the main line across the river gorge. Often to be seen standing in the halt is an 0-4-0 Wantage Tramway engine with a tram-type coach. In the station yard are a picturesque toastrack charabanc, a sporty Bugatti car and a hansom cab. A keen photographer has set his bellows camera upon its tripod to obtain a shot of the train. Down the line is a brickworks with its own works engine struggling on an incline toward Gammon Worthy Halt, with rugged cliffs above. In the centre of the widening river is Cuckoo Island upon which stands an 18th-century folly, the ruins of a Greek temple created at the behest of the former lord of the manor, Sir Hugo Gammon-Hogg.

A little way downstream the branch-line joins the main track and the two run into the village of Much Madder, where there is a boat builder's yard containing a boat under construction in a cradle. Environmentalists might be upset by the village scrap-yard with its pile of old bedsteads, tin cans, baths, car wrecks and the like. Leaving Much Madder, the line passes the Moonraker's Inn and tea-gardens and a river lock before crossing a lattice bridge, and enters Madderport, a pleasant, sleepy town which has a two-horse bus service. The station itself is the headquarters of the Madder Valley Railway but the building is unpretentious. However, at the platform one can sometimes see a curiosity of an engine from the Darjeeling and Himalayan Railway with both its water tank and its coal bunker straddling the boiler. Behind the station is the Harbour Office — a recreation of that at Poole, Dorset — and behind that the Royal Oak Dining Rooms offering a three course luncheon for 1s 9d — 9p in today's money!

The harbour itself has wharves, cranes, seamen's lodgings, pubs, a warehouse, trawlers and harbour lights. The engine shed is at the end of the town, housing the Caledonia from the Isle of Man, an 0-6-0 side tank, and Welsh Pony, an 0-6-0 saddle tank with a tender, from the Festiniog Railway. It is interesting to note that in his construction of locomotives John Ahern stretched the narrow gauge to make them fit his 16.5 mm standard gauge. Visually his licence has had very little effect on the overall feeling of realism which, though it may not match that of Pendon, still pervades this historic model.

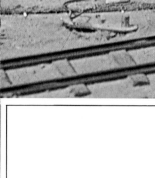

Top left: *A close-up of Pendon's* Saint Dunstan *built by Guy Williams.*

Bottom left: *Pendon's model village gives the viewer an example of Roye England's magnificent work on the construction of model buildings. This cottage is thatched with human hair.*

Above: *John Ahern's pioneering work — the Madder Valley Railway on display at Pendon Museum. This was one of the first layouts to appear as a fully scenic model.*

Fine scenery is one of the features of the magnificent working model railway which is one of the outstanding attractions of the Swiss Transport Museum on the shores of Lake Lucerne. The museum itself is possibly the finest of its kind in the world and the railway model, representing the route of the Gotthard railway along the western face of the valley of the river Reuss, certainly enhances that reputation.

The locomotives and stock used on the line are to HO scale (1:87) and are modified production models rather than built from scratch. The stock is of the kind seen on the real Gotthard line, but even with the care and attention which has been paid to overall accuracy, it has been found impossible to use trains as long as those which are seen in normal service. The locomotives are powered through overhead lines but to enable steam outline locomotives to be used as well, a stud contact system has also been installed between the rails.

Built for the Swiss Federal Railways in 1958–9 by the Lucerne Railway Modelling Club, the layout is designed as a free-standing exhibit which is enclosed on three sides by scenery with the fourth side open for easy access to the model. Its completion by volunteer workers involved more than 30,000 hours devoted to recreating in minute detail the actual line and incorporating in the model many novel features of construction which helped to overcome technical problems.

Automatic operation is made possible on the layout by a double-tracked loop layout on which trains run permanently 'north' or 'south'. Some 16 trains can run at the same time during the hourly operating sessions which are held during the season. The line, covering 380 yards (347 m), is divided into 18 block sections from which entry and departure of the trains is controlled by relays and a colour light system.

The automatic system has 40 relays but there is also a non-automatic control panel which has no less than 350 relays and 70 turnouts. This panel is made up from 'Integra' modules, thereby copying the practice of Swiss Federal Railways and serving as a good illustration of why the layout requires some seven miles (11 km) of wiring.

The actual Gotthard lines begin at Lucerne and Zurich and at a junction near Lucerne which serves towns in the industrial area around Olten and Aarau. At Arth-Goldau the lines converge and cross the Gotthard to Chiasso, near Lugano, where they join the Italian State Railways. Before the Gotthard, just beyond Schwyz, the line passes the upper end of Lake Lucerne at Brunnen and then spirals and zigzags its way over the face of the Reuss

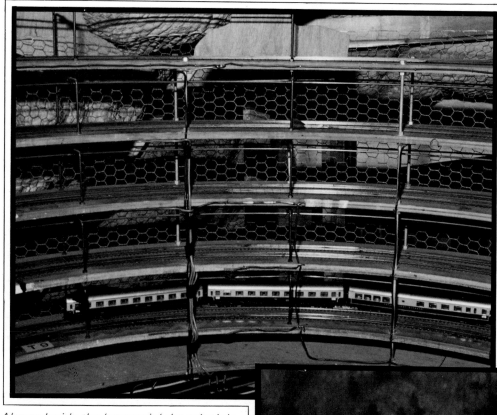

Above: Inside the 'mountain' the principle of spirals to gain or lose height is employed to bring trains from the exit point back to the starting point of their journey through the visible section of the line.

Right: The Intégra control panel from which all layout movements are initiated and monitored. The panel is identical to those employed on the full-sized Swiss railways.

Lucerne Museum Layout of the Gotthard Railway

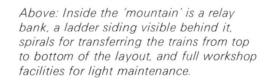

Above: Inside the 'mountain' is a relay bank, a ladder siding visible behind it, spirals for transferring the trains from top to bottom of the layout, and full workshop facilities for light maintenance.

Top: The Alpenbahn Paradies layout at
the Zurich Zoo features this impressive
scenery as background to an O gauge
layout.

Above centre: An express train with
restaurant car (which may be identified by
its red livery), climbs the northern ramp of
the Gotthard line on the Lucerne Museum
layout. The train is on the section between
Erstfeld, on the valley floor, and the
Pfaffensprung spiral tunnels.

Above: The drive mechanism of the
layout's locomotives. The power source is
AC, rectified within the locomotive to
drive the Maxon motor. This transmits the
drive by means of cardan shafts with
flywheels to twin worm drives mounted
on the bogie wheel axles.

Left: An express bound for northern Europe heads down the valley, having just negotiated the spiral tunnels at Pfaffensprung. The bridges in the background show the exit levels of the tunnel series.

Below: Car transporters await their paths in the sidings at Erstfeld. The double-banked transporters are for new vehicle deliveries; the flat cars transport normal road traffic through the Gotthard tunnel during winter when the road over the Gotthard pass is closed by snow.

Below centre: A forest of overhead wiring at the Erstfeld yards.

Bottom: One of the layout's impressive girder bridges, based on a prototype at Amsteg, above Erstfeld.

valley to Göschenen, where it enters the Gotthard Tunnel.

The model shows the line from Erstfeld to the mouth of the Naxberg tunnel near Göschenen. One side of the unit is occupied by the Erstfeld layout with the tunnels and bridges near Amsteg and the other is taken up with the Pfaffensprung spiral tunnels and zig-zagging route at Wassen, between the tunnels at Wattinger and Leggistein. Closely following the contours of nature, the model rises and falls over seven feet (2.1 m) and correctly recreates not only roads and bridges, but also buildings and rock chasms and the bemusing contortions through which the line must twist itself to reach its summits and descend again.

One would imagine that construction of the model must have presented a maze of problems, yet a look at its interior shows that ingenuity as well as standard modelling practices have been combined to produce the final, often breathtaking sense of realism. Wooden beams are used to form the basic support for the tracks and heavier exterior features of the model, and the timber is cut to approximate to the scenic contours. Across the beams wire mesh is laid to form the foundation for layers of plaster used to model the landscape. Trees and other vegetation and natural features are set into the final layer and the whole is coloured and weathered appropriately.

From the interior the tracks running in tunnels are easily accessible. The lower level of the spirals has been made into a ladder track to enable trains to be transferred or their running order altered, or for them to be taken out of service between Naxberg and Erstfeld. Here, too, within easy reach are the sidings for stock awaiting repair, the repair and servicing facilities themselves, relays, lighting fixtures and the power supply. The track is run over cork underlay which is laid on plywood bases and the HO-type rails are clipped to sleepers, one clip to every second sleeper. In fact, because HO settings have been used, the flangeways and wheels are over scale but this is only really apparent when the trains are standing in a station.

Power is supplied through overhead lines to the locomotive pantographs. The wires are 0.8 mm single strand copper where they are visible but elsewhere the tendency has been to use the stronger copper rodding. Tensioning of the wires is at approximately 1 lb per 20 feet of length and, as in real life, they are run zigzag fashion over the gantries so that wear on the bows of the pantographs is kept even. The power supply is AC rather than DC because it was found superior in keeping the rails clear of deposits of dust. Transfer of the power from AC to DC for the motors of the locomotives is done within the locomotives themselves. The motors are Swiss 'Maxons' which have their magnets fixed in a central position and the armatures wound basket-fashion around the magnets. The motor casings are used for flux return and the system seems to give considerably improved efficiency over that of the armature rotating between fixed magnet poles. It is advisable to run the 'Maxons' at their designed speeds, and to this end the locomotives are fitted with gear cages by means of which the optimum locomotive speed is adjusted to fit that of the designed motor speed. Power is supplied at between 6 v and 12v, according to the gradient which any one train is tackling and, effectively, the trains all run at a standard speed, which has the advantage of easier control of their progress through the various blocks. Flywheels ensure smooth starting and stopping.

Incidentally, observant visitors may note an unusual feature of this railway which truly reflects its prototype. Though Continental trains, like motor vehicles, run on the right, in Switzerland the railways follow the British example and run on the left. The answer to the inevitable question 'Why?' is that the first Swiss railway between Zurich and Baden was British-built and British practice has been followed ever since. A full-size replica of the first Crampton locomotive and its train is on show elsewhere in the museum.

The set trains which are used are, as previously mentioned, commercial production models which have been modified. One of the modifications is of particular interest: the original couplings have all been removed from the stock and replaced by press studs. The 'male' and 'female' halves of the stud are connected to rigid wires attached to the wagon or carriage and are simply pressed together to make a coupling. The vehicles thus remain at a constant distance apart when in motion, avoiding the danger of locked buffers and of telescoping when a train comes to a stop. However, there is a disadvantage in that the stock can only be coupled one way round — i.e. a socket must be able to receive a stud to make the coupling.

A particularly important feature of the whole unit is that it is possible to view the layout from a variety of vantage points at any angle: at eye level, close up, or from a distance, from above or from below. The perspective does not seem to suffer and the sense of realism does not seem to diminish, whichever point is chosen. From a walkway around the layout the visitor can examine its features in close detail or take in the impressive overall effect. At one point, near the Wattinger tunnel, where a stone bridge crosses a chasm, a window has been made on the side of the model and through this can be seen the inside of the tunnel. So effective is the general presentation of the model that it is possible to watch the trains wend their way through the dramatic landscape and believe that one is really standing at the actual scene.

France is now the home of a delightful model railway which was originally the work of an Englishman, William Kelly, but was presented to the Museon di Rodo (museum of wheels) in Uzès, southern France. Though it is entirely different in concept from the Gotthard it has as much to offer the modelling enthusiast. The museum contains a large collection of transport exhibits of all kinds, including a collection of over 600 railway pieces (mainly Marklin) covering the period 1896 to 1937. The main attraction in this section is the O gauge layout, named the Gur-Rug system which Kelly started building in 1923. It is the largest layout of its kind in France.

Kelly, a much-travelled railway enthusiast who was interested in English and Continental railways, located his model railway on an imaginary island in the Channel with tunnels connecting it to France and Germany. Because the intricate plans which he produced for the layout looked much like details of the human digestive system, his friends named it Gutland. The name has remained within the present-day title which is, in fact, a bi-lingual one standing for Gutland Uzetian Railways — Réseau Uzetien de Gutlande. The layout was non-continuous, with a very large, six-platformed terminus named Anatomopolis, carriage sidings, shunting yard and engine depot. The model was altered from time to time, largely because Kelly moved house several times, and during the war it was unused and lay in a shed in Hythe, Kent. However, with the return to peace, Kelly continued his work on it.

After his death in 1961 following a long illness, the collection was bequeathed to Kelly's friend, G. P. Keen, late President of the Model Railway Club of Great Britain, who later presented the entire layout, baseboards, tracks and some of the rolling stock to the Museon di Rodo. Its reassembly in Uzès was overseen by the modelmaker David Sinclair of Folkestone, who had previously dismantled and packed the layout in England under Mr Keen's direction. In its new home at the museum the layout was changed from the former non-continuous system to a new design which consisted of a large oval with four tracks, a main through station and the previous sidings, marshalling yard and depot.

Originally, two rooms on the first floor of the museum were chosen for the layout, both with a southern aspect. However, it was found that the layout would

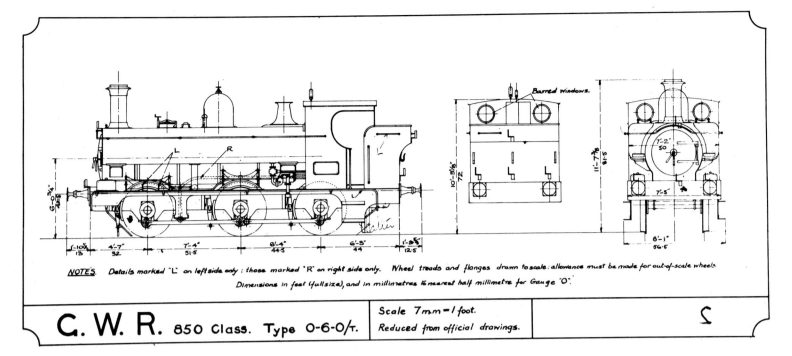

G. W. R. 850 Class. Type 0-6-0/T.

Scale 7m.m = 1 foot.
Reduced from official drawings.

2

not fit comfortably into the two rooms in its new form and some changes were called for. Rather than depart from the new design, structural alterations were made to the building itself. The station, now named D'Andoble, was reassembled in the larger room and a special gallery was constructed of reinforced concrete to carry the four tracks along the front of the building, through a window to the smaller room, and through a door into the main room again. The gallery was designed with sufficient space and strength for visitors to be able to stand in it to obtain a close look at the four tracks and a new station, Saint Quély. It was as a result of the extensive alterations which were made at the Museon di Rodo that 'Uzetian' was added to the name of the railway.

The main station has six platforms with four tracks and the four-track oval is some 130 feet (40 m) long, including its sidings, depot and shunting yard. The total length of laid down track is 380 yards (about 350 m). The scale is 7 mm per foot or 23 mm per metre and the gauge is 31.75 mm. Though most of the track is brass bullhead rail with timber sleepers dating from the 1920s, some is flat bottomed German silver rail of 109 lb/yard section scale. The 24 volt DC current is supplied through an outer third rail and is transformed by a rectifier with a 20 amp output from the 220 volts, 50 cycles of the mains current.

Six large original controllers are used on the six sections of the layout and the design is such that most of the points, except two at the new suburban station of St Quély, are in the main station area. They have been converted from the original mechanical operation to work from electric motors. Other conversion work includes a new control panel for all

A drawing of GWR 850 Class 0-6-0 pannier tank made by Colonel G. Templer and now in the Bristol Museum.

track and points electrical circuits; use of the original mechanical interlocked panel as a museum piece; improved layout with tunnels which conceal trains not actually in use and avoid any appearance of clutter on the visible tracks; the introduction of a proper scenic background with viewing windows such as that mentioned for the Gotthard model.

The Gur-Rug rolling stock is not intended to be representative of just one period; rather, it provides examples of various types of trains and periods so that visitors can see what is in effect an historical survey of railways in the south of France, and from other areas or other countries. Steam, diesel and electric trains are displayed. Similarly, the trains show examples of main-line national and international passenger traffic, suburban traffic, mail, local and international freight. The rolling stock has examples of bauxite wagons, from the small 10-tonne to the 50-tonne types, container wagons for meat, fruit, wine, trailers, an 85-tonne steam crane, oil wagons, coal and works wagons.

A short list of a few of the locomotives which are on view gives some indication of the cross-section of types:

A 4-4-2 De Glehn Atlantic with six-wheel tender, originally built by Munier for G. P. Keen's K Line and rebuilt for the Gur-Rug system;

An 0-6-2 mixed traffic 3001-3140 class PLM Railway locomotive, built in 1883 and rebuilt for the Gur-Rug with a larger cab and air brake cylinders on top of the firebox;

A Paris Orleans Railway Forquenot 2-4-2 of 1880 built by Jules Baveret and rebuilt for the Gur-Rug;

A 4-8-4 A1 class Etat Mountain engine of the SNCF by A. Chapelon rebuilt from a Marklin model;

Paris Orleans Railway 5300 class 2-8-2/T for use with mixed traffic in hilly country, built between 1911 and 1923, started by the late John Mumford (former President of the Gauge O Guild and adviser on Gur-Rug reconstruction), and completed for the Gur-Rug;

A 939-998 class 4-4-0 of the Ouest Railway of 1899 built for the Gur-Rug;

A free-lance De Glehn Atlantic built by William Kelly but altered by John Mumford for his RENFE layout and then reconverted for the Gur-Rug;

A free-lance De Glehn 4-6-0 of 1908 built by Mr Kelly for the original Gutland Railway;

A Paris Orleans 1771-1800 class 4-6-0 of 1901 as built in America by Baldwins, constructed on a Bonds chassis and fitted with a bogie tender of Hungarian State Railways type;

A Ouest Railway 2-6-2/T 3801-3850 class of 1908 which came from the Delarue-Nouvelliere collection and was rebuilt for the Gur-Rug.

Though most of the rolling stock for the Gur-Rug is now built and maintained at the system's own workshops, there are also many modelling helpers who do not live locally but contribute their work freely, so that the Museon di Rodo can be said to have national and international support.

Below: This O gauge 151 engine was modelled by Ernest Boesch after the BLS locomotive of 1913 vintage.

Bottom: P. Lottiaux designed this O gauge 121 Forquenot, modelled after the 1878 PO locomotive.

Above: Note the Hungarian Vanderbilt tender P. Lottiaux added to his O gauge replica of a 1901 ten-wheel Baldwin locomotive.

Left: Detail of a CIWL sleeping car made by Marcel Rossi in O gauge.

Right: SNCF-type electric CC7.121 O gauge by P. Lottiaux.

Possibly the finest and largest collection of Great Western Railway models and photographs in Britain is now in the hands of the Museum and Art Gallery of Bristol, in the County of Avon. Over 100 O gauge historical GWR models were first offered to the museum in 1969 by John Blissard-Barnes at a price of £7,500. This collection included a selection of models which were the work of the late Colonel G. G. Templer, of St Martin, Guernsey, Channel Isles. With the help of a grant of 50 per cent of the total cost from the Victoria and Albert Museum in London, the Bristol Museum was able to purchase the collection during the period 1971–3.

At the same time some 20,000 GWR drawings and photographs by the late Mr R. Woodfin of Tewkesbury, were presented by his family to the museum. They form an invaluable record of the Great Western to run alongside the models. It is fitting that they should have found a home at Bristol since it was a group of the city's merchants who, in 1824, put forward the first proposals for a railway to be built between London and Bristol. In fact, though John Loudon McAdam, the great highway engineer who was then Surveyor of Bristol Roads, was to have surveyed the proposed route the project was not completed. It was not until 1832 that further thought was given to railways for the city, largely to give a new impetus to the prosperity of Bristol which had been diminishing seriously. The result was the GWR Company's route to Bristol and the West of England and the coming to prominence of that brilliant engineer, Isambard Brunel. Both the company and the man are now part of Bristol's rich folklore.

John Blissard-Barnes intended his collection to be considerably more than just that; after the Second World War he set out to record in models the delightful period of idiosyncratic development which set the GWR apart from its contemporaries. The result was a collection which is so large and diverse that it would be impossible to do it justice within these pages but which more than lives up to its creator's objectives. These, according to his own words which are included in the introduction to his excellent catalogue, were 'to show the gradual evolution of the GWR standard gauge railway carriage from the short, light four-wheeler of the 1850s to the beginnings of the corridor coach era, and also to record as many as possible of the Great Western carriage livery variations which took place during the 93 years the company operated standard gauge lines'

It was, then, carriages which formed the beginnings of this historical record and the locomotives which came later — unusual in itself at that time. The carriage

models were usually worked up from photographs of actual trains which included a variety of vehicles of historical interest. Inevitably, there was some duplication but the doubles were weeded out until eventually there were some 70 vehicles, all of which were based on different prototypes and ranged from a four-wheel third class carriage of 1884 to a beautiful bow-ended corridor of 1926.

To these were added the locomotives which were selected to head a rake of carriages and to represent the types which would normally have been seen during the period represented. There is, in fact, a break from the normal to the unusual in the GWR Royal Train of 1893. Royal vehicles in the collection include the broad gauge eight-wheel Queen's Royal Saloon built in 1848–50 for Queen Victoria and converted to standard gauge in 1889. It was believed to be the first carriage in the world to be fitted with a lavatory. There, too, is the Queen's Carriage which was built at Swindon in 1873, also for Queen Victoria. It is shown as it looked in the 1893 Royal Train. The Queen travelled in the central saloon — the most comfortable and the safest position — while her dressers were in the larger end saloon and the faithful retainer, John Brown, was in the smaller saloon at the other end. The four-wheel passenger brake van No 471 which was used in that 1893 train was built in 1877 and vans of this type continued in general service up to 1929.

The smallest model in the collection is a low-roofed third class carriage of the Monmouthshire Railway and Canal Company built in 1848 and shown in GWR livery of 1880 with the stock number 1184. It was withdrawn in 1889. A fish van classified as suitable for use with passenger stock and carrying the stock number 2177 bears the code name 'Bloater' and there is also a fine 20-ton brake van from Exeter with the stock number 66810.

The models faithfully recapture the general characteristics of the company during the period as well as their own individual detail; the collection as a whole reflects the changes. The early carriages include examples of four- and six-wheeled family carriages, which disappeared from use in the Edwardian era, giving place to marvellous 60 to 70 foot corridor coaches and early dining cars. A wealth of technical information can be gained from studying the infinite details of the models, both on the locomotives and the rolling stock, and it is fascinating to note the changes in travelling habits which took place.

Mr Blissard-Barnes produced detailed notes on the models which make invaluable reading in the catalogue. They are an

indication of the extent of his own researches and observations and include personal comments based on the conclusions he drew while compiling the collection. Each model is listed in chronological order according to the date when the original prototype was built, followed by details of the dimensions, serial number and stock number, details of livery and of any changes made. Alterations such as the removal of rainstrips and their re-siting closer to roof edges were not only noted but also incorporated in the actual models. Indeed, Mr Blissard-Barnes was so diligent in his researches and his pursuit of realism that, if new facts came to light after a model had been built, it would be rebuilt not once but sometimes on several occasions to show those changes. His was work which involved constant revision as well as progression but sadly it was not completed at the time of his death in 1971. Plans for new rakes of carriages which he had made had not been carried out but fortunately he did leave the detailed notes describing his future intentions, details of current work and suggestions about where useful information on particular vehicles might be obtained.

Mr Blissard-Barnes concentrated entirely upon building the model stock and never professed to be a locomotive modeller. However, most of the better locomotives included in his collection were built to his instructions by Colonel Templer and there are other fine models by A. E. Davis and G. E. Mann of Guildford. Among these is Davis's model of Joseph Armstrong's 2-2-2 No 55 Queen of 1873, which was used regularly on Royal trains until the mid-1880s. The model was painted and lined by Mr Blissard-Barnes. Also included are a finely detailed 2-6-2 tank No 4555 by Beeson and an 0-6-0 Class 633 tank No 638 shown with the Belpair boiler which was fitted in 1923.

The collection has been increased by the museum authorities, who commissioned Mr Mann to build a number of extra locomotives. These include a Class 42XX 2-8-0 tank No 4274, one of the heavy freight engines designed by Churchward in 1910 for use in the Welsh coalfields; a Dean Goods No 2463 in the livery of the 1920s (the prototype of this locomotive served in France in the First World War and in Tunisia and Italy in the Second World War); and a Saint class 4-6-0 No 2939 Croome Court.

Visitors to the museum at Bristol should, of course, remember that the Blissard-Barnes collection was built up specifically to be seen as a static display, a museum piece in which each model incorporated authentic historic details. There is additional interest to be gained by comparing it with models built for running on working layouts. The collection was a major step forward in realistic historical railway modelling of pre-war GWR stock and it is fortunate that it has been placed on public display.

The next major step in this field was taken by the late Michael Longridge, who built many excellent 3½ mm scale models before the Second World War and turned to the 4 mm, EM track gauge as his next step in an adventurous modelling career. After the war he set to work on building a layout based on Kingsbridge in South Devon. He already knew the area from holidaying at nearby Salcombe and he now set about making a detailed study of the whole branch line from Brent to Kingsbridge. The result was one of the first modern fine scale 4 mm layouts and it is sad that his work, which, like that of Blissard-Barnes, was unfinished when he died, is not on public exhibition. However, it has at least been perpetuated by the 4 mm scale modellers of the Protofour Society.

Michael Longridge was a life-long railway enthusiast and in particular a GWR supporter. His models gained him many awards and his reputation as a first-class modeller was based on the excellence of the GWR freight stock which he produced in such loving detail. In 1938 he published an article dealing with his construction of stock from ¾ mm fine cardboard. He impregnated the cardboard with shellac varnish to give it strength and durability, using the resulting sheets to construct side and endpieces; for the floors and roofs he used satin walnut. It was his idea to form a Great Western Circle of enthusiasts. In 1945 a group of his friends got together with him to concentrate on modelling Great Western stock to a scale of 4 mm to 1 foot, at the same time proposing to meet regularly to exchange ideas.

It was not unusual in the years just after the war to see a group of enthusiasts, including the tall, bespectacled Michael, exploring a GWR locomotive depot, carriage works or yard. Inevitably he would be armed with tape measure, camera and notebook and would go to endless trouble to ensure that he obtained sufficient notes and shots. Not only was he a skilful modeller and a fine draughtsman; he was also an excellent photographer and his use of Leica and accessories enabled him to build up an important collection of photographs showing coaching stock of all kinds. Using these and his notes and measurements he made precise, beautifully finished working drawings of many of his subjects.

He also built up a coaching register cross-referenced to his library of negatives. To this work he brought the same methodical approach as he used in all his other interests, coding the entries,

dating them both as to subject and to date and place of the photographic session and the type of film which he had used. The register pre-dates his work with the group and was actually started in 1933. Apart from the war years, it runs through to 1956 and includes over 900 negatives.

It was at about the time that the group sessions began that Michael set to work on his Kingsbridge model. He first experimented with the use of ½ mm flanges on the running wheels but found that the running characteristics were far from satisfactory and that there were too many derailments. As a result he eventually disposed of all his EM rolling stock and after also selling the complete Kingsbridge layout he turned to 7 mm fine scale work.

He still did not desert the Great Western and in fact produced a superb 55XX class 2-6-2T locomotive which was electrically operated through a stud contact system. Like many other Longridge models, it has been recognised as a collector's piece. Next came a series of very fine 7 mm rolling stock models which are considered to be among the finest examples of this type of modelling.

Michael soon became famous in the world of railway modellers and enthusiasts, not just for the perfection of his work, but also because he was always ready to share with others the benefits of the knowledge he had gained and the results of the various experiments which he had made. Many of his photographs were published in the modelling press

between 1945–7 and, apart from helping to create enthusiasm in others for this scale of modelling and degree of accuracy, they were seen to be of such high quality as to be worth publication in book form. Eventually, in 1948, the small volume 'Modelling 4 mm Scale Rolling Stock' was published by Rayler and Cricklewood, largely through the persuasive efforts upon Michael of R. J. Raymond who, in 1947, was editor of *Model Railway Constructor*.

The book, unfortunately now out of print, has been described as opening up a completely new field of modelling opportunity; the average reader was shown that it was both feasible and practical to model railway vehicles in very fine detail and in very small scale. Michael once said 'Every modeller should endeavour to produce a model or a prototype that has not been modelled previously.' He also said 'You never know what you can do until you try and never, never say "That's good enough".' His sudden death in 1958 was a sad blow to the railway modelling fraternity. Fortunately much of his work is recorded in the 'Registry' which he compiled with his friend John Binney and which is a fund of authentic data on the GWR stock.

Below: A fine scale Great Western Railway 2-6-2T No 4523 in 7 mm scale gauge O by Michael Longridge.

Bottom: A GWR 1914 brake 3rd corridor in fine scale gauge O, also by Michael Longridge.

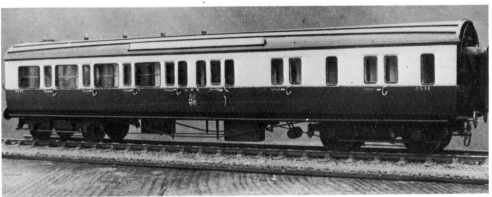

Stronachlachar

Below: The trestle bridge crossing Clackan Water is based on the Monbulk Trestle Bridge. The Clackan Water itself is made from many layers of varnish with paint mixed in it. Rocks are embedded into the stream. Cliffs are made from cork and polystyrene with assistance from Polyfilla and flock. The engines concerned are No 9 and No 5. No 9 is the Garratt, built for the Darjeeling Himalaya Railways and is hauling 25 slate wagons made from Festiniog Kits. On the bridge is the GWR built Vale of Rheidol.

Right: Beinfhada Yard modelling not finished but completely cluttered with locomotives. The white patch is a stone wall in the process of being made — it awaits scribing and painting. Not really noticeable, the track awaits ballasting and the foreground is unfinished. The nearest three lines are occupied by locomotives and the remainder by coaches, wagons and vans which were either scratch-built, kits or modified proprietary items. The locomotives, reading left to right, first row are: 2 — The John Fowler locomotive, 4 — Lynton and Barnstable, 6 — Baldwin WD engine, and 12 — an Andrew Barclay loco (GEM kit). Second row: 2 — a George England engine. 1 — a free-lance locomotive and 5 — the GW Vale of Rheidol engine. The third row has two Darjeeling Himalaya locomotives No 7, a class B 0-4-0T, and No 9, the Garratt. The other engine is No 8, a Hibberd diesel.

Below: Dearglairig station with two trains in it. The Garratt hauls a passenger train including a 'toast rack' coach modelled on North Wales quarry men's coaches. To the left of the goods shed is a Simplex-type diesel locomotive which has the driver sitting sideways; it heads a short train of tipper wagons. A short length of standard-gauge track to hold wagons carried up on transporter wagons can be seen in front of the Simplex diesel. The standard-gauge wagons on the S are hauled off by a winch. The pine-logs goods shed is scratch built; note the packing cases and other goods in the open-sided goods shed. A crofter's cottage (also scratch built) is now used as a station building, hence the awning which has been built to protect passengers from the elements. The water tower is based on the Talyllyn stone-built type. In the foreground can be seen some scouts with a handcart and their tents. Also visible is a fence style with a footpath going to another crofter's cottage.

Left: The approach to Craig Station. The narrow gauge station is visible in the foreground, while North Eastern Railway class ML 4-4-0 No 1621 runs light along the standard gauge main line, and passes a train of P.O. and N.B. wagons hauled by N.B.R. 0-6-2T No 42. The MI has a home built body on top of a chassis adapted from a Hornby Dublo GWR Castle locomotive.

Below: Alistair and Angus coaling up in preparation for the day's work. A scene on P. D. Hancock's original Craigshire Railway. Alistair is a model of one of the Manning Wardle 2-6-2 tank locomotives which used to run on the Lynton & Barnstaple Railway, while Angus is based upon one of the Festiniog Railway's little 0-4-0 saddle tanks. The tree behind the engine shed is one of a series which was marketed by Bassett-Lowke just after World War II. Each tree was individually made.

Above: A view on P. D. Hancock's 4 mm scale Craigshire — a combined pre-grouping and narrow gauge layout which superceded his original narrow gauge layout in the mid-1960s. Here a narrow gauge train hauled by Angus passes the standard gauge line which burrows under Craighill. From the tunnel storms a North British Railway Atlantic, Hazeldean, on a main line express, while in the middle distance a little privately owned 0-4-0 shunts a few vans into the siding leading to Peter Allan's Processing Plant.

Above: Alistair, a Manning Wardle 2-6-2 type, based on the engines once used on the Lynton and Barnstaple Railway, takes a train of hopper wagons past the boat-building yard at the entrance to Craig station. The tramcar in the background was also a working addition to the Craig & Mertonford Railway, which on P. D. Hancock's original layout ended up by circling the harbour.

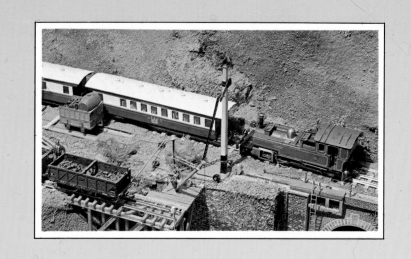

L. V. GRINSELL

Below: P. D. Hancock's Craig &
Mertonford Light Railway in 4 mm scale.
The Manning Wardle 2-6-2 tank Alistair
passes the boat-building yard at the
entrance to Craig station.

Inset: The Manning Wardle 2-6-2 Alistair
approaches Glenmuir viaduct on Craig &
Mertonford Light Railway. Narrow gauge
in 4 mm scale.

Chapter 9
In Pursuit of Realism
Home Layouts

Home Layouts

In the preceding chapter we have dealt with a few examples of model railways which are on exhibition in areas specifically devoted to or adapted for public displays. There is, of course, another breed of model railway which, though seen by fewer people, gives as much pleasure and is worthy of at least equal attention: the layouts which have been built in private homes.

Often these are the work of just one enthusiast or of a group of a few friends who spend their spare time creating and operating their railways and in overcoming those problems which are inevitably faced by anyone who sets out to design a permanent or semi-permanent layout in a private house. Awkward chimney buttresses, difficult bays and doors which somehow always seem to be built in the wrong place or to open the wrong way — these are just some of the problems sent to tax the ingenuity of the home modeller and which, in their overcoming, add to the sense of achievement.

Such a layout and one which has become a classic of its kind is the beautiful Buckingham Great Central. It is an imaginary line developed by the Rev Peter Denny from what was originally a single track line based fairly roughly on the Great Western Railway's Ashburton terminus into a complex layout handling a considerable volume of traffic and employing a computer. Originally the Buckingham project was a first attempt at 4 mm scale modelling. It was begun in 1946, more or less as a challenge to its creator; because he was not particularly familiar with the Great Central, he would have to research the subject. He was also attracted to the turn-of-the-century two-colour scheme coaches, the wooden signal posts (rather than lattice-worked girders) which presented few problems, and was a relatively unusual modelling choice.

The first layout, which was semi-portable, had a country terminus from which tracks led to Stony Stratford terminus and through Tingewick Station to storage sidings hidden from view. In fact the two stations won bronze medals at the Model Engineering Exhibition in 1947 and 1948. At the Model Railway Club Exhibition of 1948 the whole layout, which was probably one of the first 18 mm gauge two-rail layouts to be publicly exhibited, was described as one of the most outstanding exhibits. In the more than 30 years since then it has been changed many times but is now permanently settled in a room of its own, retaining the basic principles of the original.

Buckingham itself has developed into an important town and its town hall is based on the original at the real town of Buckingham. This overall development involved an interesting extension to the model, which we shall describe later in this chapter. At Grandborough Junction the tracks divide to run to Linslade country terminus and to hidden storage sidings. Though no attempt has been made to recreate an actual stretch of railway, this section represents the main Great Central line through Quainton Road and Aylesbury to Marylebone. A small branch line from Grandborough Junction to Verney Junction also ends in a hidden siding. The various station buildings were based on originals seen on the Great Central or associated companies — the arrival side of Marylebone, for example, was the basis for Buckingham Station but the roof is from Chester Northgate. No attempt has been made to build models in fine detail or reproduce exactly actual stretches of railway. However, great care has been taken to ensure that the locomotives, stock and railway 'furniture' are scale models of what would have been found on the real Great Central in 1907 — the period in which the model is set. Peter Denny has, in effect, designed an imaginary line which not only creates a series of pleasing three-dimensional pictures but is also a living working model. All of this is contained in the space of just 14 feet by 11 feet (4.2 m by 3.3 m), apart from the Leighton Buzzard extension line which runs through an adjoining room.

Three operators, one at each station, receive and despatch trains using bell codes and running to set timetables. The storage sidings are a large turntable on which trains can be turned after their arrival and held ready for their eventual return journeys. The sidings are controlled by a home-made computer working in conjunction with a clock in the Railway Room which runs at three times normal speed. Since the actual timetable represents 17 working hours, this means that about six hours of real time are required to cover a model working day.

When a train is due out from the storage sidings the Grandborough Junction operator is called by a single bell chime. After acknowledgement, the computer rings the correct code for the train, sets the points along the route leaving the sidings, and, on receipt of the line clear bell signal from the Junction, replies with 'train on line'.

If the storage sidings are to receive a train the computer again sets the correct route and will not accept it until it has received the right bell signal. Should a train be more than five minutes late in arriving or departing the clock stops and does not restart until the train is running correctly again. When only one human operator is in attendance he works from

Above and right: Great Central Railway suburban tanks by Robinson and Sacré on Reverend Peter Denny's Buckingham layout.

Buckingham and the computer is used as an operator, ignoring Grandborough Junction. The combination of the computer and the automatic clock-stopping system means that a single operator can enter the Railway Room, pick up a time-table of movement from the point at which it was left off and run the trains with the computer as an effective second 'man'.

Turning again to the interesting extension mentioned earlier, it is worth noting that this is a good example of the ingenuity to which we referred at the outset as a necessity for the modeller seeking success. It was found that almost — but not quite — every available space had been filled with baseboard for the model and that squeezing in visitors was a problem. Nevertheless, there was one area that was not being used and seemed to be going to waste: the space taken up by the opening and closing of the door! Once the door was shut there was a relatively small yet valuable portion of room which could surely be put to some use.

Peter Denny's answer was an extension flap which was designed to be

Leighton Buzzard, Linslade Station on the Reverend Peter Denny's Buckingham Railway.

raised to open the door and lowered when the door was shut. Apart from the advantage of an extra area with which to play, there was the bonus that no one could enter without permission. The particular part of the layout involved was beyond the main station buildings at Buckingham, where the buildings on the nearest side of the road were very close to the scenic backdrop and there was no forecourt. On the whole railway there was, then, no point at which the line crossed a road.

Careful study of the section provided the solution: a 20 inch long, 8 inch deep (50.6 cm by 20.2 cm) section of permanent baseboard to which could be joined by hinges another piece 20 inches by 18 inches (50.6 cm by 45.5 cm)

which would lift. On this would be a cattle market with adjacent cattle dock, served by a line crossing the main road outside the station. A spare line was available for the purpose; it had been included in a new goods warehouse in the end of which an opening was now made to run the extension through to the cattle dock. Space was even found for another siding through to serve a maltings. However, it was soon realised that it was hardly likely that wagons would be shunted by engines in steam through a warehouse to either the maltings or a cattle dock; therefore one bay of the warehouse was cut away and the whole remaining structure moved back against the backdrop. The track now ran along the new front of the warehouse in full view and a milk dock was made from a loading bank beyond the warehouse. Behind that Peter Denny added the back view of a row of railwaymen's cottages set against the backscene and including half the roof beyond the ridge tiles to give the effect of depth.

On the fixed part of the new extension a church was built which was based on Buckingham's real church but with its tower and spire moved from the west end to the centre and the nave ending against the backscene. The cattle dock, with access from the market square, has room for five wagons and it is left to assumption that the market itself is off scene, beyond the cattle pens. Another addition was the maltings, copied from those at Snape. Only part of the whole maltings is shown and again it is assumed that the line serving the visible section continues to the rest through an archway.

The church was made from wood and cardboard covered with cartridge paper which had been scored for stonework and colour washed using poster paints. The windows are of preshaped clear plastic sheeting with plastic strips cemented on them. Preshaping was done by immersing the sheeting in hot water. The effect of stained glass windows was obtained by dabbing the backs of the windows with oil colours. For the maltings the same basic structuring principles were used but the covering was of plastic sheet embossed with a brick pattern. Ingenuity again came to the fore in designing the movable section of the extension since it was necessary to ensure that when the baseboard was lifted the buildings upon it did not foul those on the fixed section. The cattle pens were set back from the edge of the dock so that the section, where the buildings had to clear the maltings when lifted, was hinged as unobtrusively as possible at the point where a bakery building joined the pavement. The neighbouring houses were joined to the bakery and, by means of an arrangement of Meccano strips, were made to slide forwards towards the town hall when lifting was necessary. This group of three houses was designed from a Lloyds Bank advertisement showing Farringdon and was built of plastic sheet finished in a cream wash. It includes the bank itself, with lettering taken from the advertisement, John Thompson's bakery, with lettering from a Hamblings sheet and from Slaters letters, and an office building.

Across the road is the town hall, built up on a hardboard base with a 2 mm plywood overlay covered with stone paper and in the busy market square, which is filled with stalls and people, stands a drinking fountain, also based on that seen in the Farringdon Lloyds Bank advertisement. On the other side of the

square are a butcher's shop, a jeweller's and a chemist's. The first is made from plastic sheet and brick paper with meat fashioned from rolled and sliced red and white Plasticine. Commercial papers on cardboard and scored were used for the roofs and were rubbed over with medical charcoal on a damp finger to give a weathered effect.

In this section, too, is the Great Central Hotel, a large building based roughly on the Yarborough Great Central Hotel and intended to complement the size of the station. It is constructed strongly with 1 inch thick, braced end walls so that it can withstand being leant upon accidentally by the operator for Leighton Buzzard section. Although Peter Denny has stated that 'no attempt has been made to build really super detail models, only sufficient detail being included that can be readily seen,' the Buckingham Great Central has become a classic example of how much realism can be achieved in modelling using care, imagination and ingenuity.

A few years after Peter Denny's first efforts in 4 mm modelling, another enthusiast decided to experiment by building a 2 foot narrow gauge line in 4 mm scale. David Mander's creation, Stronachlachar in the Scottish Highlands, which was built in a room 21 feet by 12 feet (6.4 m by 3.6 m) on baseboard 3 feet (0.9 m) wide and standing 42 inches (1.06 m) high, was started in 1952 and has also become recognised as a classic of its kind. This model was also built in a private house and again was an unusual project on which its designer had to work essentially on his own since there was then little contact among the few others working on similar lines.

It all grew from just one yard (0.9 m) of track, a wagon and an England Festiniog locomotive which originally was to have been entirely built from scratch but in fact in the end included a K's motor which was small enough to fit and came on to the market in time for its inclusion by David. Fired by the success of these first steps, he went ahead with extensions over the years: the yard of track became more than 130 feet (about 40 m), the single wagon nearly 50 wagons and 14 coaches, and additional locomotives have followed in a steady progression. The second locomotive to be built was a model of Exe from the Lynton and Barnstaple, a Manning Wardle 2-6-2T, which again was built from scratch apart from the motor and gears. This appeared in 1954 and was followed two years later by a model based on the GWR-built Vale of Rheidol engines and fitted with full Walschaerts gear. Then came a replica of the Colonial Refinery Company's 1880 Fowler locomotive, again built from scratch and accompanied by a twin built

at the same time and given to a friend of David's.

The first locomotive to take advantage of the introduction of commercial N scale items was the Baldwin 4-6-0. It runs on an Arnold chassis with a body built from scratch, Walschaert valve gear and pony truck and with the motor fitted in the smoke box. An Arnold N scale chassis was used for the next engine as well — a Hibbert four-wheel diesel for which the dimensions were taken from a photograph.

Meticulous attention is paid to fine detail in all the models, each of which usually involves some 100 hours of work. There was an exception in the case of Stronachlachar locomotive No 1, based on an Anglicised version of the Egger tank on a Minitrix chassis and scaled up to 4 mm scale. It took just two days to build at a time when David was recuperating from illness.

A superb example of perfection which is the constant aim for the Stronachlachar Railway is the Class B 0-4-0 tank of the Darjeeling Himalaya Railway built to 4 mm scale and running on 9 mm track. The fine detail of this locomotive, which has been constructed on a considerably modified Arnold chassis is a delight. It includes the rerailer bar which lies on brackets above the boiler, a lamp and bracket in front of the chimney, coal carried in the box at the rear of the boiler, an electric generator on the footplate, a sandbox over the front buffer beam and handrails round the front for use when sanding is being carried out. The painting of all the locomotives including this one, which is David's favourite, was carried out by his close collaborator, Ed Ballard, who has also put in considerable work on the scenic and architectural modelling.

Another Darjeeling Himalaya Railway type is the large Beyer Garratt which incorporates a commercial K's mark 2 motor, driving wheels and gears from Minitrains. The motor is housed in the firebox and cab, driving the four axles through a primary 3:1 gear reduction, two propeller shafts, universal joints and Minitrains worm and pinion gears. The scratch built parts included the boiler, power bogies, tank and bunker, which were machined from brass, the turned brass chimney and dome and the remainder made from nickel silver sheet and wire.

The Stronachlachar Railway starts from Stronachlachar itself, which is a mixed gauge terminus, the 18 mm standard gauge and 9 mm narrow gauge crossing a viaduct and meeting at the station. Once over the viaduct the narrow gauge leaves the standard and runs round the hillside, passing Achnachoich Halt and through a tunnel which takes it out on to the fine timber trestle bridge.

This was based on the Monbulk Bridge in the Danegong Hills of Victoria, Australia. Constructed by Ed Ballard and David Mander on a radius of 12 feet (3.6 m), it includes more than 400 pieces of stained balsa wood and is a fine example of model engineering. Thence the line runs through a rock cutting and alongside a gorge, crosses a bridge over a waterfall — based on the Festiniog iron bridge at Tan-y-Bwlch — through another tunnel bored in solid rock, along a hillside above the road which runs close to the shore of Loch Moine and over a road into Dearglairig Station.

This has a passing loop and two sidings, one of which ends in a length of standard gauge used for unloading transporter wagons carrying standard gauge vehicles from Stronachlachar. The other siding runs through a goods shed. Close by is a crofter's cottage which is now used as a station building lying parallel to the road — it having supposedly been built before the coming of the railway. Behind that is a stone water tower.

Passing rock outcrops and grass and bending now to the left again, with trees on the hillside above, the line enters another tunnel and then passes under the viaduct outside Stronachlachar Station, having completed one of its two circuits of the room. On then to Taighantulach Station, where there is also a passing loop and two sidings. One of these belongs to the Benbuidhe Quarry Company which has erected staging terminating with an unloading shoot down which granite chippings are poured into waiting barges. The staging is constructed from over 300 pieces of balsa wood. The other siding has another short length of standard gauge for unloading the transport wagons. The water tower here is of wood topped by the metal tank.

From Taighantulach the line enters another rock-hewn tunnel and curves in a semi-circle round Glen Corie, passes under the timber trestle bridge, crosses a river and enters the hamlet of Strathmoine, which, apart from its halt, has a row of cottages, an hotel and a gateless level crossing. A single timber shed forms the only station building and over the road beside a bank stands a lovely old cottage behind which is the river gorge and waterfall.

After leaving the hamlet the line crosses the Loch by way of a cob wall and enters Beinfhada Yard, which is the main works for the line. Then it crosses a river on a girder bridge, curves left again through Portbanrich town and as it approaches its terminus, splits to run on either side of the harbour of Portbanrich. The left-hand line crosses a bridge which it shares with the road over the river and enters the station where there is a treble loop with one platform between two of

the lines. The right-hand line runs along the side of the harbour and is used for slate traffic being unloaded on to ships. The scenery along the way is made from Polyfilla and commercial glass fibre fabric. Rocks and cliff faces are from cork bark and expanded polystyrene carved to shape plus Polyfilla and flock. Some of the bridges and the cob wall are made from wood formers which have been covered with Polyfilla and then scribed when dry. The excellent water effects are gained by applying many layers of varnish over the correct water colourings which have been applied underneath.

Some of the cottages are built from scratch while others, from Ballard Bros. Shops are by Tri-ang. The cottage by the river gorge at Strathmoine is built from scratch from scraperboard, while some of the row of cottages were built from scratch and others were of the kind once marketed by Ed Ballard. The goods shed at Dearglairig was built of dowel rod made to look like pine logs and the crofter's cottage which is now the station building was also built from scratch from polystyrene sheet. The stone water tower has a wood frame covered with Polyfilla into which the mortar course was scribed when it was dry. Some of the trees were shop-bought — Woolworth Christmas trees suitably doctored, for example — while others were made from scratch. At Taighantulach the station was made from a modified kit. The rolling stock is a mixture of the products, built from scratch and commercial, which have been modified; some coaches came from Egger, Playcraft and Lilliput and some, from Zeuke, have been narrowed down from metre gauge. Others are built from scratch and it is the intention to have all stock made in this way eventually. A few of the wagons are from Mike's Models and Festiniog kits while others are the work of the Mander–Ballard collaboration. Stronachlachar is one of the finest examples of the dramatic effects which can be achieved by dedication and painstaking work over a long period and of the model railway which, like all living models, continues to grow and to be a work of art at the same time.

Apart from the non-scenic display at Uzès all the models we have 'visited' in this and the preceding chapter have relied for their total effect upon the attention which has been paid by their various creators to detail, not only in the railway stock but also in the surrounding landscape and buildings. By this one does not mean necessarily the fine detail, since Peter Denny has said that his concern was more with the overall picture presented while we have seen that David Mander *is* concerned with getting the finer points right. This question of total effect is one which cannot be over-

stressed since there is nothing so disheartening as to find that having devoted countless hours to producing individual models, when put together as a single unit they do not combine to form a satisfactory, pleasing and realistic whole.

We have already dealt with some of the ways of achieving the right effects in an earlier chapter and we have touched upon some of the methods employed in the models we have visited; there are many other hints for landscapes and buildings which can be gained by reading the many excellent books on the subject. It is, for example, surprising to find how many modellers forget that weathering plays an important, one might say a vital part, in adding to the air of realism. How often can one find, even in modelling exhibitions, examples of beautifully made buildings or rural scenes which look as though they have never felt the lash of rain, the tread of feet or tyres or the merest breath of wind? How often can one find supposedly ancient buildings or cottages on which the roofs show no sign of the tell-tale sagging of age and every angle is set-square perfect? Remember always that the overall impression of a layout can be spoiled by one feature being allowed to dominate the scene either by reason of it being too large, too garish in colouring or simply by sticking out like the proverbial sore thumb because it is perhaps out of period or character.

It should also be borne in mind that a feature built exactly to scale may still not look realistic once it is set into the complete layout because the modeller has forgotten to take into account the effects of perspective, which are accentuated in modelling. This is particularly important, too, when working in half-relief, where the actual model runs into a backdrop on which the rest of its outline is painted. An example here is Peter Denny's church at Buckingham, where the west end of the nave tapers off against the backscene, and at the goods depot, where the perspective of the backscene gives the illusion of depth even though the buildings are, in fact, set against it.

Reverting briefly to the subject of angles: it is a good practice to avoid too many sharp angles and perfect right angles in a layout because, in true life, there are very few either in the vertical or the horizontal planes. Ground is rarely perfectly level and walls are not absolutely at 90 degrees over their entire faces. Nor, of course, is any surface ever a flat colour overall. Roye England's travels by bicycle across the country were not just to note details of architecture or landscape but also to study colours, light and shade.

For landscaping a wide selection of scatter materials is now available on the market and much of it is perfectly satisfactory. Some, however, have an artificial look because the colouring is too bright or is one colour rather than a variety of shades. If such material has been selected there should be no difficulty in improving it by touching it up to give the required effect for your particular purpose. Ready-packed scenic material, excellent though much of it is, does not always meet the individual's needs and a useful standby is plaster-impregnated bandages, which, after being dampened, can be laid over padding or crumpled newspaper and left to set to the desired shape. David Mander has provided an excellent example of the effective uses of cork bark for rock and cliff faces. Lichen, dyed in greens and browns and treated to remain supple, makes an excellent foliage.

Some other aids which now exist to represent the land itself are the range of polymer fillers, white glues and gouache colours, all of which are water-soluble but harden to become water-resistant and can be mixed to the desired consistency for hand-moulding to shape. In addition to sawdust for grass which we have mentioned previously, a useful aid is medical lint which is coloured with a water gouache coating and applied to the landscape base with adhesive which has also been coloured appropriately. If the lint is torn away when the surface is almost dry it will be found that it leaves behind realistic strands of 'grass'.

Though beginners may well prefer to use some of the hundreds of kits of buildings which are now available it is likely that, with experience the appeal of building from scratch will grow. Plastic models, though often of a very high standard, can sometimes look artificial, particularly under strong lighting, and despite the vast range available it can sometimes be difficult to obtain exactly what one requires, especially if the style of a particular period is involved. If building from scratch is still considered too ambitious there is much to be said for adapting a manufacturer's kit to one's own needs — just as commercial rolling stock can be satisfactorily modified or altered in scale.

When it comes to the point of putting completed buildings together to form a town, village or hamlet it is, again, as well to consider carefully the period and the type of place which is being created. Is it one of those towns which grew up haphazardly, with buildings clustered in a jumble of narrow streets running off one main street or is it a neatly laid-out, well planned place? Whichever, thought must go into the way the buildings are set down in relation to each other, remembering that even in the best planned cities not all frontages are level nor all corners neat.

Another point worth taking into account is that though they may not have been as

littered as today, streets and, indeed, railway embankments and linesides of past years were not always perfectly clean. Linesides frequently collected piles of discarded sleepers, bricks and track 'furniture' along their way and embankments regrettably became dumping places for people's rubbish in some areas; puddles, mud, stagnant ponds, straw and manure are a natural part of the countryside, too.

It is important to bear in mind that quite often railway buildings at a particular station were all designed by one man and that they therefore tend to reflect a theme. Remember, too, that roofs, which are usually prominent features in any model, need to be true to the character of the area in which they are supposed

Dinky Personnel. Hornby porters load an oversized picnic basket into a 1920's four-wheeled van.

to be set: slates, tiles and stones vary almost from one county to the next and it will not help the cause of realism of a layout if, say, buildings which are meant to be in the east of England are seen to be roofed in Welsh slate. While there are plenty of printed brick, tile and stone sheets available on the market, a useful addition to the modeller's accessories has come from increasing use of computer punch cards, the punched out 'confetti' of which makes good bricks and is even more effective for individually laid tiles, again with the proviso that these should be painted in varying tones rather than in one overall colour. Painting the tiles in one solid colour will render the work done in laying them individually meaningless.

While we are looking at the matter of achieving realism in models the question of figures and accessories which are needed to finish off a model and give it that final touch of 'life' is worthy of some thought. Once again it is period and character which matter here as much as getting the scale right. There are many excellently made figures and accessories on the market, so much so that it really is

not worth considering the business of attempting to create one's own from scratch. However, there is not infrequently a need to convert a manufacturer's model figure to suit the requirements of a particular setting. With the paints which are now available this need present no great problem, though it is worth reminding the reader who is a beginner that glossy paints should be avoided in favour of the more realistic matt.

The use of gloss on figures was, of course, commonplace for many years and indeed it can still be found today. Model railway figures seem to date back to the earliest days of mass production of toy ranges. In fact they appeared on the market when manufacturers quickly realised that model railways were in vogue. The main interest up to that time had been in toy soldiers and it was the makers of these who were not slow to appreciate the value of diversifying into the new market. Initially they seem to have concentrated on producing railway staff: porters on their own, porters carrying luggage, stationmasters and guards. However, in 1908 William Britain introduced a fuller range which, as well as staff, included station accessories' such as barrows and luggage as well as passengers. Britain & Sons had been established toy soldier manufacturers since 1893 and one imagines that the change to producing civilians presented no great problems. They were of the same size as the soldiers, which fitted well into the 1 gauge railways that were then among the most popular.

By today's standards the moulded lead figures were not usually finely modelled and they stood on thick bases which were inevitably somewhat intrusive. However, one must remember that these little men and women were pioneers for realism in their field and that today they have not only an undoubted period charm but also a considerable following among collectors. One shudders to recall the number of figures that were carelessly discarded or trampled upon.

The most important figure then was the imposing station master who, in the 1920s, was an impressive, smartly top-coated gentleman and later appeared in the braid of office, still looking suitably authoritative. Britain's gentlemen of this rank were bearded and appeared somewhat imperious. Sets varied in the number of figures — though it was usually six — but included as well as the stationmaster, a ticket collector, porters, porter's barrows and luggage. The larger sets usually also had guards with flag or lamp depending upon whether they were day or night guards; a policeman and passengers who, one recalls, always seemed well-dressed and of the upper-middle class — the sort of passengers one would have expected to see in the first class compartments;

Dinky Toys series. The range was launched with Modelled Miniatures No 1, a set of railway staff which included the stationmaster. He was described in *Meccano Magazine* as 'an imposing personage in a long coat, and his gilt buttons and braided cap are visible signs of authority. Surveying the scene with calmness, he is an impressive figure'. Also included in the set were a ticket collector with 'a business-like appearance', a guard about to wave his flag with his whistle already in his mouth, and two porters, one of whom carried a suitcase. As Hornby extended its range it became evident that the same basic moulds were sometimes being used for different characters. The porter in this set who was unencumbered by luggage, was, in his 'undressed' state, the same as the Pullman car waiter and the fitter. Suitable redecoration brought about his trans-

ladies in fashionable long skirts or, later, with fur collared coats and shorter skirts; gentlemen with bowler hats and umbrellas. Some of the gentlemen had one movable arm with a pipe in their hand, a newspaper (*The Times*?) or a Gladstone bag and an overcoat folded neatly over the left arm.

Rivalling the range of figures produced by Britain's were those of John Hill and Co which were marketed under the name 'Johillco'. They included characters similar to those of Britain's sets but differently garbed. The passengers were, perhaps, not quite so stylishly dressed, though some seemed to give a greater sense of mobility — one thinks, for example, of their small boy waving his cap at the passing train; his whole posture appeared completely natural and less 'leaden' than the general run of figures.

As O gauge became increasingly popular, Britain's, Hill's and their lesser contemporaries found that there was a call for even smaller figures. Inevitably the features on these were not defined even as well as the larger figures for 1 gauge and they relied more on the painting-in than on the actual moulding of detail. Britain's series of O gauge figures, though again based on those in the 1 gauge series, included some different characters and others who were slightly less resplendent than their larger brothers and sisters. The guard carried a flag and the passengers included a golfer in plus-fours and yellow-and-black waistcoat.

In 1931 Hornby began producing their range of O gauge figures which were to become famous as part of the

Jack Nelson's Vignette of the London & North Western Railway

Top left: West Bank Dock and Widnes Viaduct in the year 1914. The train, on its way to Liverpool, has crossed Runcorn bridge. Scale: 3.5 mm to 1 foot (1:87). Materials: polystyrene, wood, nickel silver.

Above: An untidy corner of a goods yard in the year 1914. Scale: $\frac{1}{16}$ inch to 1 foot (1:16).

Right: A typical industrial street in Liverpool in the year 1918. There was not enough space to copy a scene exactly but all the buildings are from prototypes measured before they were pulled down. The railway items include rolling stock and a typical London & North Western Railway signal. Scale: 1:16. Materials: steel, wood, hardboard, nickel silver.

formation.

The range was extended with the addition of an Engineering Set, a Train and Hotel Staff Set and a Passenger Set. The first of these three included six figures whose functions were, for example, greaser, fitter, engine room attendant, storeman and electrician. The Train and Hotel Staff included among their number that disguised porter doubling as a waiter, in company with hotel porters and a Pullman car conductor. *Meccano Magazine* described a chief Pullman car attendant in white coat and blue trousers who appeared as a responsible official with 'quite an important appearance'. His staff, similarly dressed but in shorter coats and different caps, showed 'their inferior rank'.

Among the passengers was a lady in a green coat with a voluminous white fur collar and holding the hand of a red-coated, yellow-trousered child who carried under one arm a teddy bear. Other Dinky Toy figures included another woman and child, a variety of hikers, male and female, and carrying rucksacks, a newspaper boy running with the latest edition held in one outstretched hand and his bundle of papers under the other arm, a lady carrying a suitcase and coat and another in brown coat and fur collar carrying a hat box.

All the ranges included sets with station accessories such as barrows and trolleys, chocolate machines, metal-strip printing machines, suitcases, baskets and an enormous cabin trunk (this by Hornby) which always looked large enough to defeat the efforts of the most obliging of porters.

In some ways the figures which are available today have changed very little in that the same characters are to be found. However, with improved manufacturing techniques the detail has become much finer and figures depicting movement appear more fluent. Catalogue descriptions, however, have altered and they no longer refer to 'lady' and 'gentlemen' passengers but to 'six women passengers' or 'six men, seated'. The range of people is endless and imaginative, including 'six beatniks', six drunken men', 'six corpulent passengers', 'house-wife hanging out laundry', passengers climbing and descending stairs, beach musicians and wedding guests (these all from Merten). From Merit there are a porter with an electric trolley, Scouts with a trek cart, cycles in a stand, various 'public service' figures such as nurses, policemen and ambulancemen, a seated sleeping couple, a man in a telephone kiosk with the door open (the hinge is presumably broken since he does not need to hold it in position!). There are water skiers, winter sports passengers and participants, harvesters, firemen of various nationalities. Practically every type of occupation is covered not only by appropriate figures but also with the necessary accessories. Also available are unpainted white metal figures which can be suitably dressed to the modeller's own requirements.

Some ranges continue to use stands for their figures, others are standless and therefore have to be glued in position. It is, of course, entirely a matter of personal choice as to which one uses. The advantages of figures on stands include the fact that they can be easily moved for a change of scene while, obviously, a disadvantage is that the stand can be intrusive and detract from the realism since it is by no means always possible to disguise them.

The Use of Scenery and Accessories for Special Effect

Above: Station scene on Bill Tate's O gauge coarse scale layout. Note the use of brick paper for buildings, walls and platform sides also the use of Hornby & Britain's commercially produced station staff, now collector's items. On the platform is a 'stuffed' model of the *Rocket* by Kitmaster — an excellent example of the use of accessories.

Right: Bob Ledger's O gauge Manchester Central layout. This is primarily a garden railway albeit of a transportable nature. Prototype running and rules are the byewords of this operation.

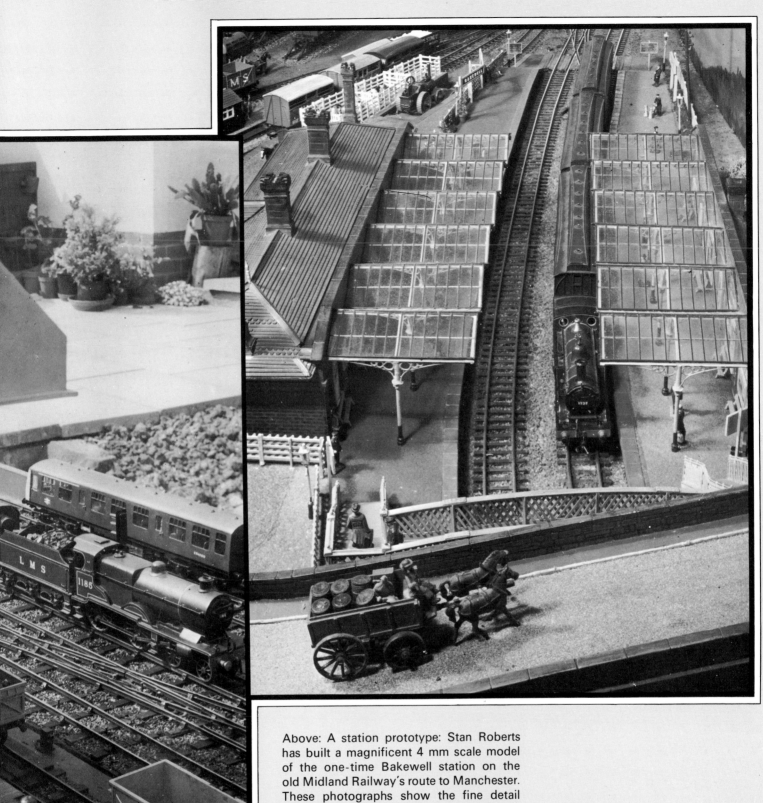

Above: A station prototype: Stan Roberts has built a magnificent 4 mm scale model of the one-time Bakewell station on the old Midland Railway's route to Manchester. These photographs show the fine detail that can be achieved with care and research. Track plans were obtained from British Railways, measurements and photos were taken on the site and suitable drawings made. The end product represents a piece of history.

Left: Railroad train ferry, an example of an unusual aspect of railway modelling. Ken Walsh built this ferry boat with an American flavour.

Below: Mickleton station buildings. Even in N scale there are graffiti experts — an example of how a little extra thought can give added realism to a layout.

Below: Commercially produced accessories can be used to the great advantage of most layouts. This Pola viaduct carries a fine model of a Lancashire & Yorkshire Railway railcar and horsebox on H. Lee's N gauge layout.

Above: One of Britain's few tubular bridges. The one at Conway is now the last of its kind. This excellent replica on H. Lee's N gauge layout based on the LMS Railway was constructed with the aid of carefully taken polaroid photographs.

Below: This village, serving Millthorpe Junction is mainly built from commercially produced Bilteezi kits. The pub and the Miner's Institute were constructed from Minitrix card.

Above: N gauge is small enough to allow a really scenic model in a comparatively small space as can be seen in this delightful picture of a Millthorpe Docks and Harbour Board 0-6-0T shunting the quay roads on H. Lee's layout based on LMS (L & Y) practice.

Right: Exterior of Cornbrook station (based on Gainsborough GCR) Manchester Model Railway Society's O gauge layout.

Left: This pithead scene is scratch built with a Peco engine shed for the winding house, a Pola narrow gauge shed for the general building and another Peco engine shed by the pithead. The screening is a Pola kit.

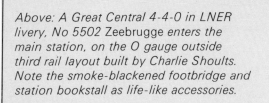

Above: A Great Central 4-4-0 in LNER livery, No 5502 Zeebrugge enters the main station, on the O gauge outside third rail layout built by Charlie Shoults. Note the smoke-blackened footbridge and station bookstall as life-like accessories.

Modelling a Group of Buildings

Ken Ball's Scale Models of Some of the Oldest shops in Macclesfield dating back to 1600 AD

The two buildings shown in the photographs utilise the same basic construction and it is in the external finish where the main differences are seen.

Initially the dimensions of the structure are drawn onto sheet plastic; then these are cut out to size, together with the door and window apertures before assembly. The walls, when joined together, are allowed to set thoroughly before the final surface is applied.

In the case of the small shop, printed stone paper was pasted onto the plastic, then when this was dry the doors and windows were fitted in place. These were made up by gluing small strips of plastic onto a transparent sheet and then cut to size. The sash windows were built up as two individual units, thus allowing for some of them to be fixed in the open position as the photos show.

Individual slates were cut from thin plastic sheet and each one fixed in place separately, but although this takes some considerable time to complete, the finished effect is amply rewarding. Gutters and downspouts are added using plastic rod. Finally the chimney pots were constructed from the sketches using thin plastic, and fixed onto their respective locations on the stacks, being firmly secured around their bases with 'Das' modelling compound which prevents accidental damage.

A certain amount of 'artistic licence' was taken with the left-hand side of the model, in order for it to fit the location on the layout, so a glass covered yard was added to this side, the idea being modelled from another row of cottages in the vicinity!!

Having completed the plastic inner shell for the row of shops, a further lamination of plastic was applied, but this time using embossed sheets. These are available in a wide range of finishes and colours.

As can be seen from the photos, embossed brickwork was used for the butchers shop, whilst the remainder was modelled in coursed stone, as per the prototype.

The only additional detail to be added to the walls at this stage was that several of the stones were 'built-up' using 'Das', to give the impression of a rougher type of stonework that was similar to the original wall surface.

Before making the many windows, these were drawn to scale on graph paper, as no two were alike in either shape or size. The glazing sheet was then secured to the graph paper and the windows assembled on top, and when complete they were trimmed to fit into their locations. Window displays were made up for each shop and glued into place before the floor was added.

By choosing an actual prototype building to reproduce in model form, a certain amount of difficulties have to be overcome in the various stages of construction, if the true character of the original is to be captured. This was certainly true in this particular case, as the front wall over one shop was fighting a losing battle of the bulge, the roofs on each one were suffering from fatigue and sagging badly, not to mention the chimney stacks leaning at alarming angles, to name but a few!! However, by suitable packing for the walls and roofs, these problems were solved, and again many hundreds of slates were added individually, each one having first been carved to shape to represent the rugged edges so common on the larger types of stone slates.

Balsa wood was cut and filed to shape for the chimney stacks before applying the embossed bricks, and these were firmly fixed to the roofs with a fillet of 'Das' to represent the cement at the base, before finally adding the chimney pots.

Top: Sketch showing general arrangement of actual group of buildings.

Below: The completed model. A comparison of this with the sketch clearly shows the faithful reproduction of the prototype, together with modifications at the left as described in the text.

Extreme right: These detailed sketches proved invaluable.

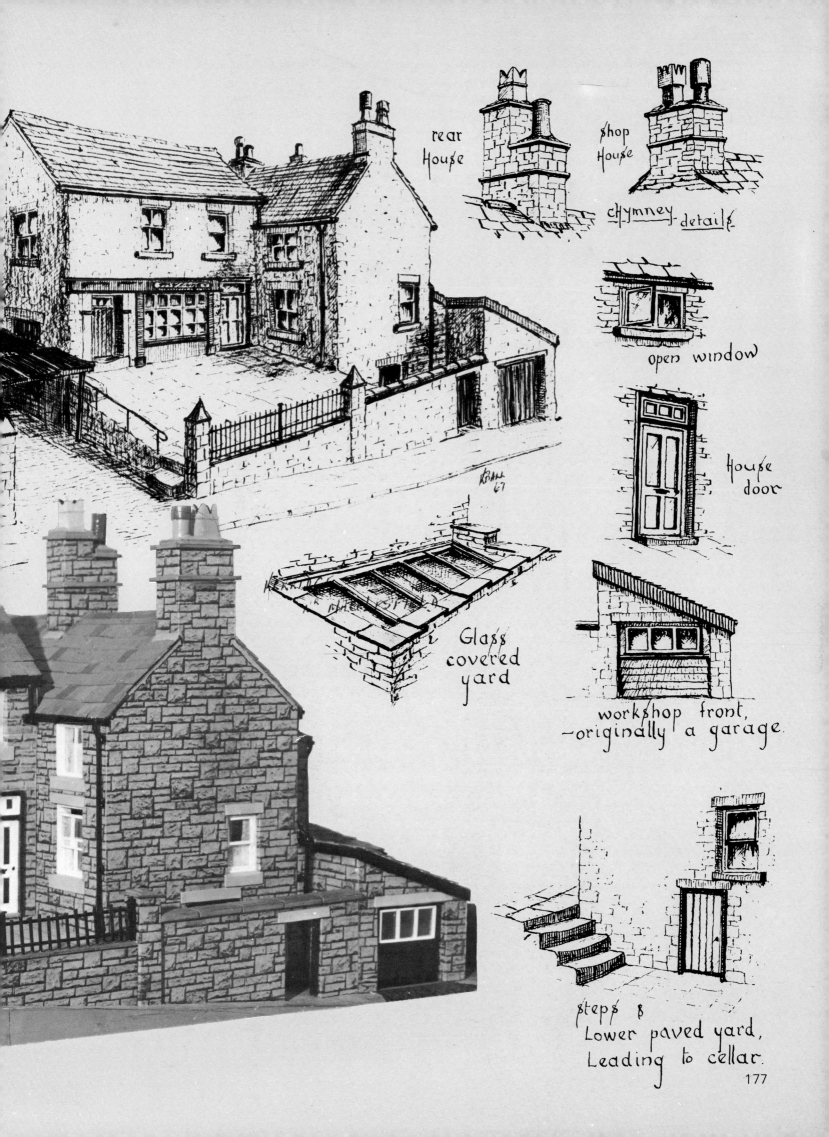

rear House

shop House

chymney details

open window

House door

Glass covered yard

workshop front, —originally a garage.

KBALL 67

steps & Lower paved yard, Leading to cellar.

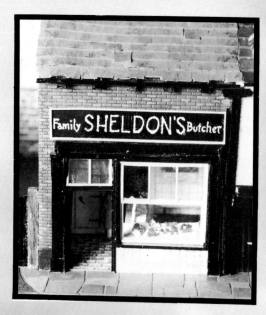

Extreme left top: Interior of this butcher's shop includes tiled floor and walls, scales, fridge and varied selection of prime cuts of meat on display.

Left: Close-up view of shop and house front. Note sash-windows, fully detailed shop interior and also young children evidently spoilt for choice with the selection on display.

Below: This group of shops in Macclesfield dates back to 1600 AD, and, as can be seen, represents a model full of character.

THE LINEN SHOP

Rene's.

Chapter 10
MODEL RAILWAY LITERATURE

Every hobby attracts the literature it deserves, and model railways have been excellently served with periodicals and books. The published word and picture is an essential ingredient in the full enjoyment of any creative activity. The various monthly magazines published throughout the world provide one of the best running surveys of the hobby, and it is fortunate that during all the key periods in the development of model railways as a major pastime, a monthly journal has been available in one form or another in both of the major model railway centres, Europe and America. It is also fortunate that the people publishing and staffing these journals have, in most instances, close ties or at least great sympathy with the subject, and there is no better example of this than in the progenitor of all model railway periodicals. This first real magazine for model railway enthusiasts commenced during the halcyon days of model trains in 1909. Published by Percival Marshall, edited by Henry Greenly with the close co-operation of W. J. Bassett-Lowke, it was called *Models, Railways and Locomotives*. It ran more or less uninterrupted until 1918 and to anybody wishing to recapture the essence of model railways during their golden Edwardian years, examples of these periodicals, either as individual magazines or bound annual volumes, are a must. While on the subject of vintage periodicals, if one is lucky enough to come across early unbound editions, which not only have covers, but also the original advertisements, never (as many people did in the past) separate this material for binding purposes. Contemporary advertisements tell us almost as much as the text, and they are a priceless reflection on how manufacturers responded to the changing patterns of demand.

Shortly after the demise of *Models, Railways and Locomotives*, W. J. Bassett-Lowke introduced the first edition of his *Model Railway Handbook* which, revised and up-dated, ran for almost 25 years.

1925 saw the birth of *Model Railway News*, once again published by Percival Marshall. For eleven years Percival Marshall was not only the publisher, but also the editor and in 1936 he handed over the editorship to J. N. Maskelyne, a legendary figure in model railways. In 1965 the Percival Marshall organisation was acquired by Model and Allied Publications, originally Model Aeronautical Press, and in 1971 the name of the magazine was changed to *Model Railways*. Relative to the model railway population, the British enthusiast was more than amply catered for as *Model Railway News* was complemented by *Model Railway Constructor* in 1934, first published by Ernest F. Carter, once again editor and proprietor. In 1959 the company was acquired by the well-known railway publishing house of Ian Allan and under this proprietorship it continues today. The last of the three main English magazines was *Railway Modeller*, which joined the fray in 1949. Since 1951, the company has been under the proprietorship of Peco Publications and Publicity, part of the internationally famous Peco Organisation, later renowned for its manufacture of 'ready-to-run' track.

The circulation figures (now *c*. 200,000 world wide) of the model railway press is an excellent barometer of the volume of interest in the subject, and it is remarkable that after a trough in the 1960s, model trains have climbed back to enjoy even greater popularity than before. This is even more significant in view of the immense growth of alternative proprietary hobby products, namely plastic model kits of all kinds, radio-controlled models and, somewhat spasmodically, slot car racing. The popularity of model railways is even more astonishing when considering the run-down of the real railroad system both in the United States and in Europe, and as a general rule the lack of glamour afforded to trains throughout the world. The answer to this odd correlation must lie with the psychologists,

but in terms of longevity in a world given to embracing the latest fashion, the continued commercial success of model railways as a major international hobby is all the more remarkable.

The buy and sell columns of the model railway press are another highly useful source of information and a definite market-place for the enthusiast. Many people initially become involved with the hobby through answering one of the many classified advertisements carried regularly in each magazine. Apart from periodicals, the model railway hobby has also been served by specialist publishers who have, over the years, given the enthusiast a commendable library of excellent source books. Again with one or two notable exceptions, these books tended to centre on the 'how to do it' aspect. In the past few years, however, no doubt due to the enormous growth in the collecting side of model railways, more publications dealing with historical research have appeared. Many of these have taken the form of reproductions of original source material, principally manufacturers' catalogues and one publishing house is even reprinting its early and extremely rare in-house model railway magazines. Of the former type of book, once again Henry Greenly's name appears with great prominence. His first book, *Model Steam Locomotives*, was published in 1914, to be followed in 1922 by *Model Electric Locomotives and Railways*. Gustav Reder, the doyen of European collectors wrote *Die Modell Eisenbahn*, first published in 1926, but alas only in German. Edward Beale's classic *The Craft of Model Railways* and *Scale Railway Modelling Today*, published in the 1930s, can still be read not simply as a nostalgic exercise, but as a series of much concrete information which is still relevant to today's hobby. Rather like the steam locomotive itself, the appearance may have changed dramatically over the years, but the principles grasped by the early pioneers remain surprisingly constant. Edward Beale was also to collaborate with Frank Taylor (then editor of the pioneer American *Model Maker* magazine) to publish *Model Cars and Locomotives* in 1940.

The first serious publication, devoted almost entirely to HO/OO railways was E. W. Twining's *Indoor Model Railways*, published in 1937. Dealing principally with how to integrate scenery with a layout was P. R. Wickam's *Scenic Railway Modelling*, put out in 1944 and, reflecting the scarcity of metal model material at the time, E. Rankin Gray's *Cardboard Rolling Stock and How to Build It* — as with so many books, the lessons of building with card are still valid today. J. H. Ahern, a master model railway builder wrote three classic books, namely *Miniature Building Construction* (1947), *Miniature Locomotive Construction* (1948) and *Miniature Landscape Modelling* (1951). In 1950, Ernest F. Carter attempted the impossible by writing a model railway encyclopaedia which unfortunately, like most of its genre, is weighed down by its name, and regrettably requires significant revision if it is not to fall into the trap of merely being a huge and ponderous snapshot of the knowledge of this particular subject at a specific moment.

During the 1940s and 1950s two books were published in the United States which stand like beacons in the world of model train collecting. The first was entitled *Riding the Tinplate Rails* (1944) by Louis Hertz. It is a marvellous intimate romp down the tinplate years, written by a man whose opinions contemporary manufacturers often sought when making important decisions on product development. Louis Hertz is unique in the annals of the hobby in that he brought (and still brings) a degree of scholarship, erudition and overwhelming application to a subject that had hitherto not appeared to have drawn in an intellect of this magnitude. Reading *Riding the Tinplate Rails*, whatever your nationality or interest, will bring you to the essence and even the inner secrets of the amazing popularity of model railways. Louis Hertz's second classic — passing over his *Messrs Ives of Bridgeport*, (1950), his own favourite but nonetheless a specifically American history of that legendary firm — *Collecting Model Trains* (1954) came at a time when the collecting hobby was getting into full swing and the need for guidelines and criteria arose. Louis Hertz provided all this and more, and while this book is written almost exclusively for the American collector, its conclusions are universal. It is hoped, one day, that these books will be printed again in their original form, without too much revision, for they encapsulate all the enthusiasm of the pioneering days of the hobby and

should not be diluted with the mass of facts which have since come to light.

In Europe Hamilton Ellis, the well-known railway artist and historian, wrote a charming and somewhat whimsical work entitled *Model Railways — 1838/1939* (1962). While lacking the scholarship of Louis Hertz or Gustav Reder, it was nonetheless an excellent read for the layman and enthusiast alike. The next landmark in this specialised field was Gustav Reder's *Clockwork, Steam and Electric*, first published as a German language edition in 1969 under the title, *Mit Uhrwerk, Dampf und Strom*. Like Hamilton Ellis's book, it dealt with the period up to 1939 which, as discussed earlier, appears to be the generally accepted cut-off point when deciding whether or not a model train qualifies for the description 'vintage'. In 1974 came the first comprehensive pictorial history of commercial railways, *A Century of Model Trains* by Allen Levy. This book earns its place in the history of the hobby by being the first to give the collector or layman a retrospective glimpse at the amazing diversity and charm of model trains and incorporates more colour and black and white illustrations than had previously appeared in one single publication on this subject. As with so many things, synchronisation was at work in that shortly before the publication of *A Century of Model Trains*, New English Library set in motion a massive part-work, entitled *The History of Model and Miniature Railways* under the editorship of Patrick Whitehouse. The publication of this highly popular weekly partwork seemed to underline the fact that model railways now enjoyed a significant and growing following and could no longer be regarded as a rather strange and eccentric minority pastime.

Another entirely independent source of published information comes, of course, through the medium of model railway manufacturers' own catalogues. These are of enormous importance and whereas original copies may be rare, the collector is well served by the publishers who in recent years have reprinted many of the key manufacturers' classic catalogues. A comprehensive list of these is given in the bibliography.

Curiously the continent of Europe has been less well-served by the model railway press and this may, in part, reflect the greater popularity of 'ready-to-run' systems and their reliance on manufacturers' literature. Nevertheless, some notable magazines are the French *Loco Revue* and *Railway Miniature Flash* and in Germany *Eisenbahn (Modelbahn)* magazine and *Modell Eisenbahner and Miniatur Bahnen*. Both Fleischmann and LGB publish their own house magazines and these are a mixture of prototype railway

practice and surveys of their own in-house products.

Prior to 1934, there was no recognised model railway press in the United States, and this state of affairs accorded with the relatively small group of people who were building their own model railway equipment during the 1920s and early 1930s. Europe it seems, and particularly England, was at that time way ahead in the field of 'do it yourself'. The popularity of ready-to-run model railways dominated the American scene, and by their very nature 'ready-to-run' systems do not of themselves require a separate model press. The colourful catalogues and house literature of the various manufacturers servicing this market were almost a body of literature in themselves and they were usually free! Articles concerning model railways did, however, appear in an American journal called *Model Maker* which commenced in 1924. In fact, much of the early HO enthusiasts' literature and equipment came from England, the first and last time that English-made railway equipment was to penetrate the US market to any real extent. For an in-depth survey of the American 'How to do it' publication I highly recommend Paul Mallory's excellent article in *Model and Miniature Railways*, Part 35.

One of the pioneers of American model train track was William K. Walthers who in 1932 wrote a significant book entitled *Signal and Control Manual for Model and Miniature Railways*. In 1933 the first edition of *Model Craftsman* was published, although this really started life as a general hobby magazine. A few years later it became predominantly a model railway magazine, and devoted virtually its entire content to the hobby, changing its name to *Railroad Model Craftsman*. The publishers of this magazine published a classic handbook which is still an incomparable source of information. In 1934, the first 'all model railroads from the start' magazine was launched, named *Model Railroader*. Both these magazines continue to thrive today and indeed, *Model Railroader* magazine, published by Kalmbach, put out a unique survey of the model railroad hobby in America in 1969. At that time they estimated that there were over 150,000 active hobbyists in the United States. Their interest in various gauges was broken down as follows:

Gauge	Percentage
HO gauge	76.7
N gauge	12.7
O gauge	6.8
S gauge	2.3
TT gauge	0.4
all others	1.1

They further determined the occupations of model railroaders as follows:

Occupation	Percentage
Professional	25.2
Students	20.8
Skilled workers	15.8
Executives	10.9
Government employees	7.2
Salesmen	5.5
Self-employed businessmen	4.7
Clerical	4.6
Teachers	2.8
Retired persons	1.5
Unskilled workers	0.9
Farmers	0.1

The following questions concerning the model railway hobby were posed, which are as relevant today as they were then and, indeed, the reader may well with some benefit question himself in a similar way:

1. Is this really just for fun?
2. Can I afford this hobby?
3. Do I have the health for it?
4. Do I have the space for it?
5. Can I do this alone?
6. Can I do this with others?
7. Do I have a special talent for this?
8. Have I the time for it?

Further statistics which underline the long-held concept that railways are certainly not only for children were tabulated in a general distribution of age survey:

Age	Percentage
11 years and younger	0.3
12 years	0.8
13 years	1.9
14 years	2.6
15 years	2.4
16–20 years	9.0
21–30 years	31.2
31–40 years	26.0
41–50 years	14.6
51–60 years	8.4
61 and older	2.8

It is fair to say that if one applied these statistics to the collecting hobby then the age band would, if anything, widen to include collectors between the age groups of 31–40 and 51–60. The survey further determined that the best-liked areas of the model railroad hobby were as follows:

Area	Percentage
Bench work	8.8
Signalling	1.2
Control and wiring	5.8
Scenery	6.9
Armchair (reading about other people's efforts and attending clubs)	8.9
Structure construction	12.9
Locomotive construction	13.8
Car (or Coach) construction	19.8
Train operation	21.9

One area where the American hobbyist, (owing to the nature of American housing) is significantly better off than his European counterpart is in the provision of basements which usually extend under the full area of houses in the United States. Over half the modellers in America indicated that their permanent layouts were located in the basement, whereas only some 4.5 per cent were located in the attic. The reverse would probably be true for the UK.

One final statistic which has probably not materially altered over the intervening years either in the USA or Europe is the period preference, although the emphasis has by now probably shifted slightly more towards the later periods.

Period	Percentage
Very early models up to 1865	0.8
1865–1900	8.0
1900–1935	46.0
1935–1960	13.8
The 1960s	9.3
No preference	22.1

Whereas there is no substitute for practical experience and, more important, learning by your mistakes, the new and old model railway enthusiast should take full advantage of the marvellous body of literature which is the fruit of tens of thousands of hours of building, re-

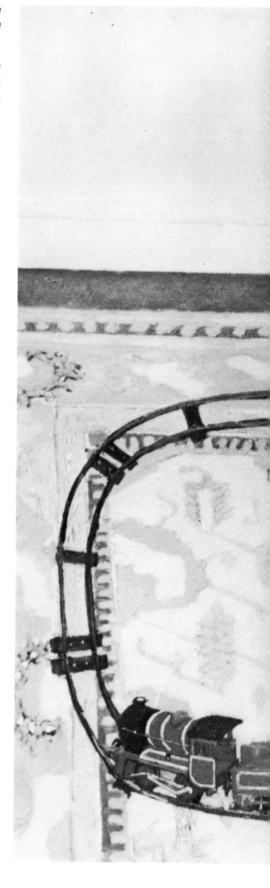

Trains in Art. *This picture by Claude Rogers of the Camden school, was entitled simply 'The Hornby Train'. Whether father would normally sleep during 'train time' is by no means certain!*

searching and collecting. As in so many areas, other people's ideas and experience are there to illuminate your own.

Clubs and Societies

The readership of any piece of literature, particularly periodicals with their correspondence columns and classified advertisement sections, tends to form the readers into a loose affiliation of like-minded people. However, in any pastime, the more committed will tend to seek out other interested people on a more formal and structured basis. In some cases this coming together is a purely local or regional affair and the local model railway club or society is always an excellent jumping off point for the beginner or, indeed, any enthusiast who derives great satisfaction from the companionship of other like-minded individuals rather than spending every spare moment on his own projects. Many people become totally involved with their club or society and find this more satisfying than the obvious restrictions that must apply in a purely domestic environment. Apart from regional affiliations, there are, throughout the world, several national and international groups and undoubtedly the most prodigious are those in the collecting field. As might be expected, America boasts the largest of these groups, namely the Train Collectors' Association of America or TCA as it is more commonly known. At the time of this writing their headquarters at York, Pennsylvania, are in the course of being turned into a permanent and large scale museum of working and static exhibits. There are also specialist national organisations such as the Hornby Railway Collectors' Association (HRCA), which are only concerned with one manufacturer's products. There is, too, a Marklin Club being formed in America on a similar basis. Most of these organisations issue their own literature and the HRCA, in particular, publishes a monthly magazine which acts as a powerful link between its far flung members. Current lists of these and other organisations can always be obtained from the editors of the various model railway periodicals. There are many societies and associations concerned with promoting a particular scale or gauge. Many of these are mentioned in the table of scales and gauges (page 86/87) and apart from issuing newsletters, data sheets and bulletins, several also publish handbooks which outline the purposes and standards of the particular group. Most of these groups are affiliated to the international association for model railway standards, the National Model Railway Association (NMRA). The designation NMRA is often used in its own right when describing such characteristics as wheel flange thickness as being up to NMRA standards.

183

A realistic goods yard showing the use of
proprietary Hornby Dublo and stock.

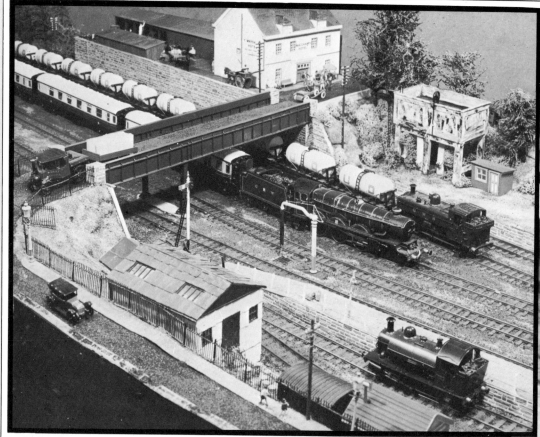

Great Western Railway in Miniature

Above: West end of Totnes station on the Castle Railway Circle's 4 mm scale GWR layout based on Totnes in South Devon, England. In the foreground is a 1363 class dock tank, centre is Castle class No 7007 Great Western and, in the milk bay, 0-6-0 pannier tank No 7700.

Right: A good example of a lattice footbridge.

Top: General view of the East end of Totnes station with GWR tank No 7700 and mogul No 6367.

Above: Totnes station. The building in the background is a model of the one-time atmospheric pumping station now in use as a permanent way store.

Left: East end of Totnes station. On the left is 2-4-0T No 459 bringing the Asburton branch train and in the station is 4-4-0 No 3824 *County of Cornwall*.

ACKNOWLEDGEMENTS

Brian Monaghan: 38/39, 130/131.

Brian Monaghan courtesy *Railway Modeller*: 2/3, 64 (both), 68 (both), 69 (top 2), 70/71, 77 (top), 82/83 (all 3), 91 (bottom), 104 (all 3), 105 (top), 108 (bottom), 109 (all 3), 110/111 (both), 112/113 (all 8), 128/129, 130 (top left), 154/155 (both), 170/171 (all 3), 172/173 (all 5), 174/175 (all 4), 176/177 (all 3), 178/179 (all 3), 184/185.

Brian Monaghan courtesy *Model Railway Constructor*: 42/43, 46/47, 76, 77 (centre), 80, 87 (top), 94/95, 98/99, 102/103, 106/107, 114/115, 134/135 (both), 136/137, 160/161.

New Cavendish Books: 12/13 (all 3), 16/17 (all 3), 18/19 (all 3), 20/21 (all 4), 22/23 (both), 24/25 (all 3), 26/27 (both), 28/29 (all 3), 30/31 (both), 32/33 (all 3), 37 (both), 40/41 (all 3), 44/45 (all 3), 48/49 (all 3), 75 (top), 91 (top), 124/125, 192.

E J Gulash: 50/51 (all 5), 52/53 (all 3), 54/55 (all 3), 56/57 (both), 58/59 (all 5), 60/61 (all 4), 92 (bottom), 120/121 (all 5).

Colourviews Limited: 11 (top right and bottom), 14 (top 2), 34 (top left), 34/35 (bottom), 116/117, 154/155 (all 3).

John H L Adams: 10/11, 38 (top left), 62/63, 88/89, 138/139, 143.

Ron Prattley courtesy *Railway Modeller*: 65, 66/67 (both), 96/97 (all 3), 186/187 (all 5).

Philip Kelly courtesy *Railway Modeller*: 72, 81 (all 3).

P D Hancock: 132/133, 156/157 (all 4), 158/159 (both).

Peter Williams: 14/15 (bottom), 74/75, 140/141, 142 (both).

J Joyce: 122/123, 126 (both), 169.

P B Whitehouse: 8/9, 15 (top).

The 2mm Scale Association: 78/79 (all 7), 108 (top).

Malcolm Cross: 144/145 (all 3), 146/147 (all 7).

Museon di Rodo: 150/151 (all 5).

Shigeki Ohyama: 4/5, 6/7 (bottom).

Junichi Yoneyama: 7 (top).

Jack Nelson: 166/167 (all 3).

Bristol Museum: 149

New English Library: 34 (top right).

Courtesy Faller: 35 (top).

The Central Press Photos Limited: 36.

K Keyser: 119 (all 4).

J H Delaney: 69 (bottom).

Peco: 118.

Tony Hall-Willis: 92 (top).

Mr & Mrs Nixon: 73 (both).

C J Freezer courtesy *Railway Modeller*: 93 (all 5).

D Jenkinson: 105 (bottom).

Dick Ganderton: 87 (bottom).

J H Russell: 153 (both).

Ronald Doyle courtesy *Railway Modeller*: 162/163 (both).

D B Denney: 164

The author would also like to thank Stewart Hine who drew all the line illustrations used in this book.

BIBLIOGRAPHY

Only books and magazines that are currently available or were recently in print are listed here. The more important or long-out-of-print historical books have been referred to in an earlier chapter.

Periodicals

France: *Loco Revue*
                Rail Miniature Flash
Germany: *Eisenbahn (Modellbahn) Magazine*
                Modeller Eisenbahner
                Minaturbahnen
Switzerland: *Eisenbahn Amateur*
U.K.   *Model Railways*
                Model Railway Constructor
                Railway Modeller
U.S.A.   *Model Railroader*
                Railroad Model Craftsman
                Railroad Modeller

Books

Alexander, E. *The Collectors' Book of the Locomotive*, Clarkson N. Potter.

Andreas, M., *OO Gauge Model Railways*, Almark Publications.

Andreas, M., *N Gauge Model Railways*, Almark Publications. (Almark also publish a related series dealing with railroads, tracklaying, track-planning and landscaping techniques.)

Baecker, Carlernst and Haas, Dieter, *Die Anderen Nurnberger*, (Volumes 1–5) Hobby Haas.

Baecker, Carlernst, Haas, Dieter and Jeanmaire, C., *Marklin Technical Toys Over the Course of Time*, (Volumes 1 & 2. There are a further 8 volumes in this series to be published.) Hobby Haas/Verlag Eisenbahn.

Carstens, Harold H., *The Trains of Lionel Standard Gauge Era*, Railroad Model Craftsman.

Cowell, Case, *Toy Trains of Yesteryear*, Model Craftsman Publishing Corporation.

Ellis, Hamilton, *Model Railways 1838/1939*, Allen & Unwin.

Freezer, F. J., *A Home for Your Railway*, Peco Publications.

Godel, H., *Antique Toy Trains*, H. Godel (Privately sponsored publication).

Greenberg, Bruce, *Greenberg's Price Guide to Lionel Trains (post war)*.

Greenberg, Bruce, *Greenberg's Price Guide to Lionel Trains (pre-war)*.

Greenberg, Bruce, *Full Colour Reproductions of Lionel Catalogues 1923–1946 (individual)*.

Greenberg, Bruce, *Lionel Catalogues, 1903–1917*, Greenberg Publications.

Hare, Burke, and Wolken *Toy Train Treasury: (Volume 1 – The Vicar's Collection Volume 2 – La Rue Shempp Collection)*, Iron Horse Publications.

Hertz, Louis, *The Toy Collector*, Funk & Wagnalls.

Hornsey, Pat (ed), *An Introduction to Model Railways*, New English Library.

Huntingdon, B., *Along Hornby Lines*, Oxford Publishing.

Jeanmaire, C. (ed), *Bing 1902–1904*, Verlag Eisenbahn.

Jeanmaire, C., *Bing, Grandad's Model Railway*, Verlag Eisenbahn.

Jeanmaire, C., *Die Weiten Spuren (Railway Models of Marklin)*, Verlag Eisenbahn.

Jenkinson, David and Campling, Nick, *Historic Carriage Drawings*, Ian Allan.

Joyce, J., *Collectors' Guide to Model Railways*, M A P.

Levy, Allen, *Bassett-Lowke Railways*, Bassett Lowke (Rlys).

Levy, Allen, *A Century of Model Trains*, New Cavendish Books.

Levy, Allen (ed), *The Great Toys of George Carette*, New Cavendish Books.

McComas and Tuohy, *Collectors' Guide and History to Lionel Trains*, (Volume 1 – pre-war) TM Productions.

McComas and Tuohy, *Post-War Lionel Trains*, TM Productions.

Minns, J. E., *Model Railway Engines*, Weidenfeld & Nicholson.

Randall, Peter, *The Products of Binns Road*, (6 volumes yet to come) New Cavendish Books.

Rorke, F. J., *Historic Wagon Drawings, Historic Locomotive Drawings in 4mm Scale*, Ian Allan.

Reder, Gustav, *Clockwork, Electric and Steam*, Ian Allan.

Stevens-Stratten and Carter, *British Mainline Diesels*, Ian Allan.

Thomson, Vivien, *Modelling Period Buildings*, Peco Publications.

Whitehouse, Patrick and Adams, John (ed), *Model and Miniature Railways*, New English Library.

Williams, Guy R., *The World of Model Trains*, Andre Deutsch.